T0161138

*By buying this book you are directly supporting
the mission of Green Card Voices.*

"The guides of this book are the very children honestly sharing their journeys in their own words. Their lessons are the lessons of America—past, present, and future. Courage, hope, determination, pain, hardship, and dreams of a better future—all are present afar and now in Minneapolis, MN. By paying attention to their testimonies, we all have a chance to reclaim and recommit to the promise of what America was when they were far away—and help them collect today, in person, on the very protections that we are so proud of when America is at its best."

—**John C. Keller, Executive Director,** *Immigrant Law Center of Minnesota*

"Every story held powerful life lessons for me—and I think all readers may have the same experience. This fantastic collection of memories, hopes, and dreams will inspire readers to never forgot that we all are truly 'in this together.'"

—**Mark Ritchie, Former Secretary, State of Minnesota**

"The migrant crises in the Middle East, as well as Central America, Europe, and Africa, are ongoing and have put refugees in the headlines. Yet in report after report, countless human tragedies are reduced to mere numbers. Individual stories such as these add a face to the news, touch our hearts, and lead to greater understanding in a way that newscasts and headlines can't. By experiencing the discomfort, fears, and triumphs of these individuals, these immigrant stories resonate especially strongly at this moment of ongoing refugee crises and shed light on immigration here in the US and abroad."

—**Judy A. Bernstein, Author,** *They Poured Fire On Us From the Sky: The True Story of Three Lost Boys of Sudan*

"This book is an important intersection of two great things: high school students writing at a rigorous level for all of us to enjoy and a beautiful elevation of the voices of recent young immigrants from which we all can learn."

—**Eli Kramer, Executive Director, Hiawatha Academies**

"*Green Card Youth Voices* speaks eloquently with the innocence and authenticity of young people finding their way in a strange land—our land. By reading these moving stories, we enter their world and begin to understand the challenges they face, and we emerge with profound respect for who they are and appreciation for what they add to our lives and our culture."

—**Charles F. "Chic" Dambach, Former President, Alliance for Peacebuilding**

"Honesty, heartbreak, and hope fill the pages of *Green Card Youth Voices: Immigration Stories from a Minneapolis High School*. It's a beautiful and important book. Read it. Share it. Celebrate the power of their words to inspire us all."

—**Tracy Nelson Maurer, Author, Children and Adult Fiction/Nonfiction**

"This book gives a voice to young immigrants navigating high school in Minnesota. Their reflections are harrowing and matter-of-fact, recalling wars and gangs, displacement and refugee camps, hunger and lack of opportunity. Revealing their hardships and hopes in broken syntax, this book reminds readers of the privilege of nonimmigrant status. It shows this country's painful flaws to a young population enthusiastic about the opportunity for an education and the chance to contribute to society and to help their community. There could not be a better time to share these stories."

—Dr. Brenda Kayzar, Urban Geographer, University of Minnesota

"Immigration is about so much more than immigration. It is about America's past and our future. *Green Card Youth Voices* gives young immigrants an opportunity to share their stories and their hopes for the future. These are our neighbors, our classmates, and our friends. Listen to what they have to say."

—Trista Harris, Philanthropic Futurist

"*Green Card Youth Voices* is one of the most powerful collections of authentic immigrant voices I've ever come across. Within these pages you will find the hopes, dreams, and sheer fortitude of our country's future innovators and teachers. Their words will impress upon you the very fabric of what has made our country a beacon of hope for so many across the world. I look forward to sharing this anthology with my students and teachers—the stories in *Green Card Youth Voices* are inspiring and will empower communities around the nation for years to come."

—Sylvia Beevas-Smith, Principal, Best Academy Middle School

"*Green Card Youth Voices* helps amplify voices we might otherwise never hear. It gives us a rich human look at who we are as a modern society, and how we can learn to live better with those who have recently arrived in this country."

—John Noltner, Founder, A Peace of My Mind

"Powerful! In a cultural era where immigrants and new Americans are under attack, *Green Card Youth Voices* provides a fresh and positive voice for the diverse experiences and dreams of kids in our community. Real experiences. Real kids. They are the future for this country."

—Dr. John Moravec, Author and Founder, Education Futures LLC

Green Card Youth Voices

Immigration Stories from a Minneapolis High School

Zaynab Abdi, Luis Angel Santos Henriquez, Ayan Arbow, Mohamed Abdiwahab, Nanah Jalloh, Willian Alonzo, Zamzam Shukri, Yonis Ahmed, Jennifer Nuñez Paz, Abdulahi Osman, Nathaly Carchi, Kayd Falug, Zamzam Ahmed, Yonis Yusuf, Dorette Nguelefack, Khadar Muhumed, Jennifer Erraez, Abdinasir Hussein, Safiya Ahmed, Aksum & Tsion Woldeyes, Quan Guan, Abdirahman Hirad, Alexandra Irrazabal, Ikrem Nuru, Wendy Saint-Felix, Fosiya Hussein, Eduardo Lopez, Keriya Hassan, Ahmed Ahmed

Authors

Tea Rozman Clark and Rachel Mueller
Editors

ISBN 13: 978-1-949523-00-3
eISBN 13: 978-1-949523-01-0
LCCN: 2016940155

Printed in the United States of America
First Printing: 2016   Second Printing: 2019
20   19   18   17   16   5   4   3   2   1

Edited by Tea Rozman Clark and Rachel Mueller

Cover design by Elena Dodevska
Interior design by José Guzmán and Shiney Her
Photography, videography by Media Active: Youth Produced Media

Green Card Voices
info@greencardvoices.org
www.greencardvoices.org

Consortium Book Sales & Distribution
34 Thirteenth Avenue NE, Suite 101
Minneapolis, MN 55413-1007
www.cbsd.com

This book is dedicated to the twenty-nine young people in these pages, to everyone they've left behind, to those with whom they've been reunited, and to all the others who join them on their journeys.

Table of Contents

Foreword

This year, I've been teaching at North Hennepin Community College. I accepted the opportunity because I understood that I would be teaching young people like my cousins and myself. In my classes, I've met many white students; the majority of them are Post Secondary Enrollment Option students, and a small minority are American veterans trying to make good on an education the government promised them when they signed up to be men and women of war. In my classes, I've met many people of color, men and women, young and old, who have traveled far to call this place home, struggling to learn English and living lonely lives in cold Minnesota. I've learned from each of my students, but it is in the voices of those who are yearning to belong, to find themselves in the literature we are reading, desperately piecing their stories into English on the pages before them, that remind me of why so many people, the world over, make the long and often painful journey to America, imperfect as it is.

A Hmong boy in my Hmong American Literature class told me that he didn't realize he was different from his white peers until he was in the fifth grade and a teacher asked the class to draw a picture of themselves. In his self-portrait, the young boy carefully mirrored his round face, his almond eyes, the slant of his brow, his button nose, and his side-swept bangs to the best of his ability. To make sure that all who looked upon the image would know it was him, he even included the gold chain with the cross he wore around his neck each and every day. When the boy was happy with his picture, he showed his teacher. She looked confused for a moment and then said, "I told you to draw yourself." The boy pointed to the page, the familiar features, and the gold chain. The teacher shook her head, frustrated. She said, "You're not white." This was the first time the boy realized that Hmong was different. Since that moment, he has been looking to find pieces of his story in the books in the classroom, to find pieces of himself, to no avail.

A young man from Somalia in my From Immigrants to Refugees class responds to a writing prompt—"What is your American dream?"—in a series of heartbreaking moments. He had a plane ticket to go anywhere in the world, and he chose Ethiopia. I asked, "Why?" He answered, "It is the closest I can get to Somalia." In a presentation about his return to Ethiopia, he shared a memory from his youth: "When I was a boy in Somalia, I had to walk two hours to get a meal from the United Nations. Sometimes, I was so hungry that I walked too slow, so by the time I got to the center the food would be gone. I would return home. I couldn't go to sleep. My grandma used to tell me to put rocks in a piece of cloth, twist it up tight, and weigh my stomach down so the growling would cease long enough for me to fall asleep. I ate banana peels when we were lucky." In a forum conversation, he wrote, "I am living my American dream. This is what young boys, hungry and afraid, dream about: a full stomach, a chance at education, the opportunity to work beyond dreams."

A woman from Liberia in my Writing Composition I class can barely write in English. The guidelines were simple: a one page, double-spaced, 12-point font response to a short story she read for class. The page before me was a jumble of language, in 9.5 font, single-spaced, no indentations, full of incorrect grammar, spelling errors, punctuation mistakes.

I asked, "What is this page about?"

"It is everything important to me," she answered.

"What is important to you?" I asked.

"That is the story of my life," she said.

"Why are you writing the story of your life?" I asked.

"It is the only thing I want to do in English," she said. My job is to help her.

My year at North Hennepin is coming to a close. I cannot take my students with me; instead, it is their stories that will accompany me.

In this book, you meet stories like those of my students. You get to carry them with you—these young people who've traveled so far, from so little and so much, to try belonging—and fortify your heart, your journey, and perhaps even your dreams for this life we share in America. In these pages, you get an opportunity to push away the walls of your life and let the world enter, through the eyes of its youth, through the stories of how it is that we are born in different parts of the world but are still connected by the fabric of humanity and hope.

Kao Kalia Yang
Award-Winning Author of *The Latehomecomer: A Hmong Family Memoir*

Acknowledgments

In the fall of 2014, Green Card Voices (GCV) exhibited its first 100 immigrant stories at the Intermedia Arts Gallery in Minneapolis, Minnesota. The exhibit was visited by a large audience of educators and students and consequently toured many schools, including Wellstone International High School in 2015. Katie Murphy-Olsen and Tara Kennedy, current teachers at Wellstone, were among those who saw the exhibit. They approached GCV and shared that they had a pressing need for their immigrant students to see positive role models and the stories of people like them. Taking this idea a step further, Katie and Tara imagined a project where their students would share their own stories, an empowering process with the added benefit of informing many more students and teachers. We were very receptive to their idea as it would help us more accurately reflect the immigrant population. At the time, there were only two youth stories in the GCV collection. As Chimamanda Ngozi Adichie states, "The single story creates stereotypes, and the problem with stereotypes is not that they are untrue, but that they are incomplete. They make one story become the only story." Having more stories of young people seemed critical.

After reaching out to the Marbrook Foundation for funding, GCV contracted with the Media Active team of Intermedia Arts and recorded thirty stories from immigrant students of Wellstone High School in Minneapolis, Minnesota, in September of 2015. These courageous youth, coming from thirteen countries, sat with Executive Director Tea Rozman Clark in the studio for several days and shared stories of family, school, change, and dreams. After recording their narratives, we knew that this was bigger than our typical video interviews. We, in consultation with the publisher Wise Ink and the Wellstone students and teachers, wanted to go a step further and bring these stories to an even wider audience with a powerful book and video multimedia package. We hope the book will be a vehicle to generate awareness and take the stories outside the all immigrant classroom. Developing this book inspired GCV to begin a Youth Empowerment Program that began with students partnering with professionals to gain new skills (e.g. video editing and public speaking).

We could not have completed this project without the dedication, enthusiasm, and hard work of the teachers and staff at Wellstone International High School. They brought this project to life. Katie Murphy-Olsen, Tara Kennedy, and Daniel Aamot worked with students in their classrooms and one on one to help them move their stories from transcripts of their video narratives to polished essays. Bob Peterson, the media specialist, helped with logistics and was a major advocate throughout the process. Joyce Vanderscheuren recruited students to participate in the project. These teachers were the bridge between Green Card Voices and the students, and we are forever grateful for their commitment to helping their students share their stories. Thanks to Maria Henly, a longtime Wellstone volunteer, for working with the students in the writing center. Thank you to Principal Aimee Fearing for creating a school environment where projects like this can thrive. Finally, thank you to Minneapolis Public Schools.

We are humbled by the breadth of support we've received in realizing this project.

141 contributors from five countries and eight US states were key in helping us reach our funding goal through an online crowd-funding campaign. Thanks to these generous individuals, we can use this book as an effective and sustainable tool for change. Through book discussions, the study guide for classroom use, and the book's online dimension, we hope these students' words will be powerful voices for many years to come. We extend deeply heartfelt gratitude to all those who helped make this project as big as possible.

Through a matching grant, generously donated by the Minnesota Twins, we were able to meet and go beyond our funding goal. A special thank you goes to contributors Ashley Wirth-Petrik, Dara

Beevas, and Melissa Persson and to journalist Erin Hinrichs for her article in MinnPost that helped spread the word about *Green Card Youth Voices*.

Thanks to the Best Buy Foundation and our graphic designer/ video editor, Jose Guzman, for co-editing the videos with the students. Because of the grant we received, Jose was able to help the students build twenty-first-century skills utilizing new technology through film editing. He designed the beautiful interior that presents these stories in a rightfully engaging manner.

A tremendous thank you goes to Dara Beevas and Patrick Maloney at Wise Ink Creative Publishing for their advice, support, and encouragement. Our collaboration as well as their donations of time and consultation through the InkPossible program greatly enhanced the final product.

Veronica Quillien, who is also the lead author of *Voices of Immigrant Storytelling: Teaching Guide for Middle and High Schools*, is a PhD student in the Curriculum & Instruction Department at the University of Minnesota. We thank her for her expertise in designing the study guide and for creating the accompanying teacher workshop. Thank you to Kathy Seipp and Amy Schuler for reviewing and editing the study guide and making it suitable for educators.

To Joseph Voelbel, Abdi Roble, Nausheena Ali Hussain, and George Maxwell, we thank them for the care they put into researching and creating the glossary. Thanks to Zoe Nardone for the huge amount of time she put into transcribing and creating videos and working with the students.

Thanks to Rachel Mueller, who coordinated the crowdfunding, edited the stories, and navigated the publishing process, moving these narratives from spoken words to tangible pages.

Tea Rozman Clark guided the project and provided the leadership necessary for this book to realize its fullest potential. Her guidance and commitment to the vision motivated everyone involved to create this inspiring collection.

There are many individuals who have been critical in the creation of this book and many more who have shown unwavering support. Our work has thrived due to their tremendous encouragement and support. We would like to thank our Green Card Voices Chairman of the Board, Miguel Ramos; board members, past—Ali Alizadeh, Laura Danielson, Angela Eifert, Arlene Hornilla, Ruhel Islam, and Okokon Udo—and present—Hibo Abdi, Jeff Corn, Johan Eriksson, Jane Graupman, Matthew Kim, George C. Maxwell, Faraaz Mohammed, Kathy Seipp, and Veronica Quillien—and all others who have helped our mission along the way.

Introduction

Immigration is an important symbol of the United States. Immigrants have played a vital role at each turn in our nation's history and continue to do so today. Green Card Voices (GCV) captures the life stories of recent immigrants in order to build a bridge between immigrants and nonimmigrants from across the country. This is accomplished by sharing the firsthand immigration stories of foreign-born Americans and portraying the "wave of immigrants" as individuals with interesting stories of family, hard work, and cultural diversity. Through digital storytelling, GCV presents a rich collection of narratives that illustrate the immigrant experience. Utilizing an open-ended interview methodology, GCV provides a platform for immigrants to tell their own stories in exactly the way they want to be heard. This book is an extension of that idea and focuses on the greatest resource America has—its youth.

The youth of America is the future of America. As the stories in this book show, based on the resilience, bravery, and courage that the next generation carries, we are in good hands. In a time when immigration to the United States is increasing—by 2050, one in five Americans will be an immigrant[1]—it is more important than ever to create a culture of empathy and appreciation for the rich diversity of experiences immigrants bring.

This book would not be possible without the thirty student authors from Wellstone International High School. Their courage inspires us all; they are the heart and soul of this work. Through their efforts, we are able to transcend boundaries and learn about the truth of the human experience.

One student's story involved walking through the desert without food or water. Another student experienced frostbite during his

1. Camarota. "Projecting Immigration's Impact on the Size and Age Structure of the 21st Century American Population" Center for Immigration Studies, 2012.

first winter in Minnesota. Many have lived their childhoods away from one or both parents. They have lost loved ones, lived in refugee camps, ridden the tops of trains, attempted suicide, and contracted tuberculosis. Their reasons for immigrating are vast, but a common thread unites them; despite tremendous tribulation, these young people continue to work toward the futures of which they dream.

The broad range of experiences these youth bring, and the honesty with which they tell their stories, is empowering a generation that will work to build a nation where all voices are heard and valued. We could not be more thankful for their contribution.

We hope that *Green Card Youth Voices*, with the study guide and glossary, will be an invigorating resource for English and social science classes, adult learners, EL classrooms, and book clubs. It is relevant, contemporary, and written with the genuineness that is unique to young people. Our most recent immigrant population has yet to see itself represented positively in society, especially within our systems of education. This book acts as one way to remedy this unfortunate reality.

How to Use this Book

At the end of each student's essay, you will find a URL link to that student's digital narrative on Green Card Voices' website. You will also see a QR code link to that story. Below are instructions for using your mobile device to scan a QR code.

1. Using your mobile device—such as a smartphone or tablet—visit the App Store for your network, such as the Apple Store or the Android Store. Search the App Store for a "QR reader." You will find multiple free apps for you to download, and any one of them will work with this book.

2. Open your new QR reader app. Once the app has opened, hover the camera on your mobile device a few inches away from the QR code you want to scan. The app will capture the image of the QR code and take you to that student's profile page on the Green Card Voices website.

3. Once your web browser opens, you'll see the digital story. Press play and watch one of our inspirational stories.

STEP 1

Download the app.

STEP 2

Scan the QR code.

STEP 3

Watch the digital story.

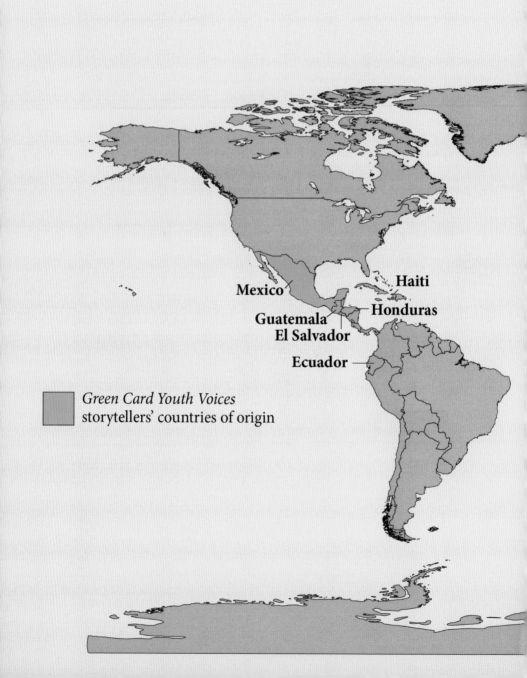

Mexico

Haiti

Honduras

Guatemala

El Salvador

Ecuador

Green Card Youth Voices
storytellers' countries of origin

World Map

China

Yemen

Ethiopia

Somalia

ra
Cameroon
ne

Kenya

Personal Essays

Aden, Yemen

Zaynab Abdi

From: Aden, Yemen
Current City: Minneapolis, MN

"WHEN I CAME HERE, IT WAS SUCH A DIFFERENT LIFE THAN WHAT I'D SEEN IN MY COUNTRY OR IN EGYPT."

My name is Zaynab Abdi. I grew up in Aden, Yemen. I grew up with a big family. There were eleven members in the same house. I grew up with my grandma from my father's side. I have seven sisters. My grandma died in 2010. When she died, I didn't want to live there alone, so I decided to move to the United States. Before I decided to move to the United States, the revolution against the president in Yemen happened. There were a lot of problems, so I decided to move to Egypt. I moved in 2012. I stayed there two years because I got sick. I had TB. After that, a revolution started in Egypt too. Then I moved to the United States in 2014.

I came to the United States because my mom had been here for sixteen years. She had a chance to come to the United States by lottery. She came here, and she couldn't take us because she had to be single to come. After sixteen years, my sister and I decided to come to the United States.

When we moved to Egypt, the embassy there accepted me, but they didn't accept my sister. I came directly from Egypt to here after two years. My sister, Sabreen, could not come with me to America because the ambassador refused her visa. I came by myself. During the 2015 school year, my sister talked to me and told me that she would travel to Europe by boat with many immigrant people. She said that it would be safe because they took a lot of money from them. That was the worst risk that she decided to take. She and some of my family

1

moved from Egypt to Italy. They arrived there after seven days. I did not hear anything about her for one month. I was afraid that something would happen to her. Now she's in Holland, but she's still finding a way to stay in the country and to be accepted as a refugee.

I went to school when I was in Yemen. I loved school and my classmates. I was not that clever, but I was a hard worker. I could not finish my education because of the revolution that happened in Yemen. During the war between the people and the government, we lost our houses and our people. My relatives and my friends died in the indiscriminate bombing in our area. I was very scared, and I wanted to hide from the soldiers. Me, my sister, and some of my family decided to move to Egypt. After one month of living in Cairo, Egypt, our neighbors from Yemen told us that our house was destroyed because of the bombing.

I grew up with my grandma and with my father's family. I loved them so much. I had a beautiful life there. We had a simple life. Our neighborhood was the best neighborhood. We didn't have much money, but we shared the good things together. We had parties at night. The neighbors came to our house because we were their only neighbor that had TV at the time. So they came and watched with us. I had my friends come, and we played games from our culture. The neighbors brought their food to share with us. I loved my life there. I wish I could go back.

When I got the visa, I moved from Egypt directly to Minneapolis. My mom, she came and picked me up from the airport. It was direct. I didn't take any risks, so I didn't lose my way. When I came here, it was such a different life than what I'd seen in my country or in Egypt. I was seeing people that were different than our people. It was cold, it was winter . . . I didn't get used to cold weather. I liked it so far. It was a nice country.

After that, sometimes I was sad. I wanted to go back to my country because I didn't like people here. They didn't like me, or they didn't like to talk to anyone. I was smiling at them, trying to open conversation, but they would cut the conversation short. After two months, I decided to continue and make my own goals while I am in the United States.

It takes much more than a month to get used to these new things. I went to school, and I saw many more opportunities that these kids in America had in their schools than my school back home. They have lunch during the school time, but in my country we used to bring our food with us. Some kids did not have money to bring food every day. In America they also have teachers and people helping them with their homework, but in my country you have to pay money for extra help. I liked everything here, and I told myself that I had to take advantage of all these opportunities in this place to get better in my future. In my country there is no future even if you finish college. Most of the college students end up being cleaners at restaurants or having no jobs at all. I had a chance to work here and make some money. I loved the life here.

I came on December 8th, and after two days I attended school. My mom showed me the directions from my house to school, and she let me go by myself. It was the best thing I'd ever done. I was walking in the street in a different country. I was looking at new people, and they were looking at the way I was dressed. Then I was like, "Okay, let's do it." I went to school, and I saw the students were not that much different because they were immigrants like me. They were from Somalia, Latin America, China, France, and around the world. So it was nice meeting them. I found one person from Yemen too. I felt like I belonged here. This is my area.

I hadn't seen my mom for sixteen years, so it was different. My culture and my mom's culture are different, so I had to get used to American culture and my mom's culture because she is from Somalia, and I grew up in Yemen. When I came here, I attended high school, and I made my own goal. I went to an internship, STEP-UP, and I said I wanted to try to be a lawyer. I started the internship for law at University of Minnesota. I did my best, but I was so confused because my English was so bad, and I was still new in the country. But when I did my best, out of thirty students, I got in the top three. It was the best thing ever. I was like, "Whatever my language, or even if I am an immigrant, I can do it." So in the future I want to be a lawyer.

I am now working at a law firm as a file clerk. After the STEP-UP program finished, my supervisor at work asked me to work with them. She told me that I was a good worker and they wanted me as an employee.

I am a senior, and I applied to many colleges. One of the colleges I applied for was Harvard because Harvard has an awesome law school. One day I want to graduate from Harvard Law School and become the best lawyer ever.

I live in a house with my mom and my two sisters; they were born here. That's the first time all of us have lived together. I would like to grow up here and finish high school and college too and then go back to my country to build my future there.

I want to say that when any immigrant person comes to the United States or to Europe or to any country, it doesn't mean that they hate their country or that they just want to try a new country. Maybe they didn't find a chance to complete their education, or maybe there were problems and war. So when they move to another place, another state, another country, they need that safety, and they need their future. One day every immigrant will go back to their country and build it because they belong to their country.

VIDEO LINKS

greencardvoices.org/speakers/zaynab-abdi

San Salvador,
El Salvador

Luis Angel Santos Henriquez

From: San Salvador, El Salvador
Current City: Minneapolis, MN

"I REMEMBER THAT I WAS LOOKING AROUND AND EVERYTHING WAS SO DIFFERENT AND I WAS LIKE 'WHERE AM I?'"

People from the LGBT community face a lot of challenges in El Salvador. A lot of people from the LGBT community come to America as a way to escape from the dangerous situation in El Salvador. Many of us had to come here illegally. In my case, it was different; I got the opportunity to come here without worrying about my legal status. Sometimes I see this opportunity as a gift from God.

I was born in San Salvador, the capital city of El Salvador. My life has been really tough since I was a child. I have faced so many challenges—with my family, society, and people around me. Since I was four years old, I was bullied because of my sexual orientation. In my house, there were always problems with my dad and my mom. They used to get into fights a lot.

My parents transfered me from one school to another because things changed. Sometimes they got more expensive, so they wanted to find a school that was cheaper for them. It was really hard for me to find friends, and I used to get bullied every single day because of how I looked and all that.

I got to a point when I was thirteen years old that I tried to commit suicide. It was really hard for me because I didn't have the support of my family. You know, people were just throwing hate and hate on me. I was like, "I don't know what to do. I need something to really get out of this." I was telling my mom that I needed help because I was getting crazy in those thoughts and thinking, "I wanna die, I wanna

7

die, I don't wanna be here anymore." Things changed later on, and I started to have a better relationship with my parents. My mom and my dad started to understand that this is who I am, and they cannot do anything to change it. Having their support makes me stronger in facing society. It was really tough at the beginning, but things got better.

My coming to the US started when my grandma sponsored my dad. But when Barack Obama won the presidency, there was a law that people that were under twenty-one were able to come with their parents. So I got onto the same traveling visa. That's how my dad and I came here.

When I first got to the US, it was really hard for me because I didn't have a good relationship with my dad. We didn't use to see each other really often. He was kind of a stranger to me. At the beginning, I didn't know what to do because I didn't know my dad really well. I was missing my mom so much. I remember thinking this world was so different from my country.

I didn't used to speak any English. It's been hard for me to understand another language, and when people talk to me, sometimes I get lost, and sometimes people think that I am crazy because I can act in a different way when I don't understand something. I remember that I was looking around, and everything was so different, and I was like, "Where am I?" I was always wondering how life would be here. But I knew that it would be better than in El Salvador. Here, there is less homophobia and transphobia. People from the LGBT community get to live a better life here than in El Salvador.

I remember when I first got here, my grandma and my aunt were two of the most helpful people. A day before my school year started, they showed me the way step by step to get to the school from my house and vice versa.

Now I will say that I feel comfortable speaking English; I know Minneapolis, Minnesota, really well, and I feel good living here. I feel safe. I feel so safe that I don't even want to go back to my country. I know that if I go back there, something could happen to me. There have been a lot of problems with homosexuals and transsexuals; they get killed every single month. A large amount of people get killed because of their sexual orientation. I feel really good living here in the United States.

I would like to have my mom here in the future, and I would also want to be a psychologist and a cosmetologist. Those are the things that I really love to do. When you are talking to a psychologist, if you have a problem, they can help you solve that problem by talking. A cosmetologist can help you look better, and if you look better, you will feel good.

When I think about things that I had to give up, one is my education. If I was in El Salvador, I would be almost graduating from college. Here, I am still in high school.

Now I am working and going to school. I see things differently than I saw them at the beginning. I feel that somehow, now that I am well adapted here, I don't want to leave.

VIDEO LINKS

greencardvoices.org/speakers/luis-angel-santos-henriquez

Jilib, Somalia

Ayan Arbow

From: Jilib, Somalia
Current City: Minneapolis, MN

"WHEN I WAS IN KENYA, MY MOTHER TOLD ME OUR WHOLE FAMILY WAS GOING TO AMERICA. MY FAMILY WAS VERY HAPPY..."

My life in Somalia was so-so. First it was good, and then Somalia started fighting. Life was changing and becoming bad. Then we moved from Somalia to Kenya.

Kenya is a very good country. They helped my family and me. I only went to school for three months because I didn't have money for school fees. In Kenya, I had my family. I had to work a little bit to have money to help my family. I was working with vegetables outside in the market. I worked by myself. One bad thing about Kenya is that it is hard to get money. After that, we moved from Kenya to America.

When I was in Kenya, my mother told me our whole family was going to America. My family was very happy; we were going to a good country that has school and everything.

In Kenya, at orientation, I learned about how America is and its behaviors. It was good. We watched videos. I saw houses. I saw how to clean the bed and the house after breakfast. We learned that Americans don't like animals in the house, like mice and little animals touching the plates.

I moved from Kenya to Pennsylvania, and then we moved from Pennsylvania to Minnesota. I was only in Pennsylvania for three months. I cannot tell you about Pennsylvania because I stayed inside. Minnesota is good, and I started school at Wellstone High School. I was pregnant, and right now I have a baby. That's good. I'm happy because I'm learning in school.

Oh, it is different in America. There are beautiful buildings. Everything is good. I see many Somali people in Minnesota. In Pennsylvania, they have few Somalis. I feel so happy when I see other Somali people in Minnesota.

Outside, in Minneapolis, it is safe. But one day I was on the bus—a black woman on the bus said to me, "What are you doing? This is not your country. Go back to your country." I was so angry. I did nothing but be quiet. I do not like the bus. I have a car, and my brother Mohammed drives me where I need to go.

My life now is a very good life. It's the best life because I have work, I have enough money, and I am good. My baby is going to daycare, and I am going to school. I have everything to help me. I feel good. My work is cleaning houses. It's not hard.

For the future I want my baby, my son, to live a good life. I want to be a nurse, and I hope to finish school.

VIDEO LINKS

greencardvoices.org/speakers/ayan-arbow

Addis Ababa,
Ethiopia

Mohamed Abdiwahab

From: Addis Ababa, Ethiopia
Current City: Minneapolis, MN

> "SOME PEOPLE DREAM ONE DREAM; SOME PEOPLE DREAM A LOT. I DREAM A LOT."

My name is Mohamad. I was born in Ethiopia. I lived in Ethiopia for seventeen years. I was already a refugee there; I am Somali. Ethiopia has different religions; we have some Christian people, and I am Muslim. I lived in a refugee camp. Some people helped refugees. We were given food and sugar, but we didn't have work. You didn't have to buy things if you stayed a refugee. We waited one month for food. After that, we waited another month for food. That's a hard life. Some days we had work, and some days we didn't have work. That's a hard life for a refugee. Some of us didn't have lunch or breakfast, some children were hungry, and some didn't have water. Some people had water, breakfast, and lunch, but didn't have a good house. Some people had work or money, and then they had to buy a new house in the market. Some people stayed refugees, and some people moved to other countries. Some were searching for work, for life. That's my life.

I have a big family. My family has nine people. All are younger, and only I am older. I have six brothers; they are all here in America with me and my one young sister.

I remember my country. I remember my friends, and I remember my city, and my school, and my teachers.

We were waiting there in the refugee camp for many years, waiting to go to the United States. In refugee camp, we had a post. We wrote our family name on paper, and then we went to that post and checked what time we would fly. Then I went to my family and said,

"Oh hello, Mom, tomorrow we are going to the United States."

"Oh really?"

"Yeah, we should." Then we were all happy. Then we came to the United States. We had to go to the airport at eight o' clock to wait to go to New York. Then we went from New York to Chicago and from Chicago to Atlanta. We stayed in Atlanta for three months. Then I went to summer school—I think for two weeks or one week—and then I stopped going to summer school because I saw some people working. Then I started working. Then some people called and said we should come to Minnesota. They have a Somali community. "You need help. We have help," they said. Then we moved to Minnesota, and there were many Somali.

I saw it was beautiful outside, and there were beautiful houses. It was different—like the bathroom. We didn't have a bathroom. For refugees, it was different. You only used the bathroom, you didn't use the shower. I saw the shower, and I saw many things were different. I said, "Wow! You have everything."

I didn't know how to speak or how to buy things. I didn't know how to go shopping. It was hard. I didn't know how to talk. I went to school, but I was quiet. But I came here, and some people were helping, telling me, "You say it that way, you say it that way . . ." Now, I've learned more English. That's why I came to Minnesota.

Now I go to school at Wellstone International High School. I took last year and this year—one year and a half. I've learned many things. I hope, in my future, to graduate, go to university or college, and then to get a job. Then I want to help my parents, or my friends, or some people, like refugees. That is my dream. Then I'll get married, and then I'll have children.

I like soccer. I played with Wellstone last year and this year. We won the last three games. I had three goals. In each game, I had one goal. I like soccer. That's what I do now.

I want to play soccer, like Cristiano. I want to do that for the United States. That's my dream. We have different dreams, right? Some people dream one dream; some people dream a lot. I dream a lot. It's not just one dream. I dream to be an engineer or doctor or a professional player. That's my dream.

greencardvoices.org/speakers/mohamed-abdiwahab

Freetown,
Sierra Leone

Nanah Jalloh

From: Freetown, Sierra Leone
Current City: Minneapolis, MN

> "MY HOPE FOR THE FUTURE IS TO LET THE PEOPLE WHO SAY I'M NOT GOING TO END UP GOING TO COLLEGE SEE ME WALKING THE STAGE AND LET THEM BE PROUD OF ME."

My name is Nanah, and I'm from Sierra Leone. I have been living in a city for my whole life. My mom left when I was one. I stayed with my dad from age one to age twelve. My dad got me some school uniforms and ironed them, and he kept my socks and shoes clean because in Sierra Leone my private school had rules about that. My dad also taught me how to get dressed and helped me do my homework. He was a nurse and worked at his own pharmacy. He had his own pharmacy because my mom sent money to him to open it.

My mom didn't see me for a long time, so she wanted me to come close to her so I could meet her and we could know each other. She told my dad that she wanted me to come to the United States with her, and then my dad told me the plan for me to move. The day when my dad told me that I was gonna come here, I was not feeling good about it because I was used to my dad. My dad had to talk to me. We went to Senegal for my visa, and they asked me questions. Some of the questions I didn't know, but they said it was okay because I was young. One lady let us come the next morning to get my visa. We went to go get a visa, and we came back to Sierra Leone, and I was crying because I didn't want to leave my dad.

Sierra Leone is the place that I wanna live my whole life because there's a depth to the place. I am used to it there. Sierra Leone is a country where there's a war; sometimes there are rebels that come and fight the people, killing people, because the government does not take care of the people. I never saw the war, but my family told me about it. When my mom was pregnant with me inside her, she had to run away from the war. Also, the government just uses the money for themselves. They don't take care of the people—the poor people. There are diseases and all that. My mom was scared about all that, and she sent me to America.

When I first came here, I didn't like it. I was not used to the food on the airplane. I didn't eat; I was just scared. When I came, my mom told me that I had to go to school. I was kind of nervous. I was starting sixth grade. My first day of school I was just quiet, and one girl, she came by me, and she said, "Hi, are you new?"

"Yeah," I said. I didn't want to talk to anybody because I was not used to anybody.

"Welcome," she said. "You can be my friend if you want."

"Okay," I said, so we went outside and played.

That same day, after school, my mom took me to Valleyfair, a place with many rides to have fun. I was kind of scared of the rides because I was like, "Nah, I'm gonna fall."

But she said, "No, you're not gonna fall. They're gonna put seat-belts on you." I went on the ride, and I was kind of crying, but it was fun. Other days my mom picked me up and we went to the mall, went to the State Fair, and all that. It was fun. I liked the chicken, cookies, and corn at the State Fair.

I didn't like the snow. The day when the snow started, I came out to go to school, and it was freezing because I had to wait for my bus. In Sierra Leone, I took a taxi to school every day, and I waited for the taxi in my family's house. I didn't like waiting outside in the snow. I told my mom I wanted to go back to Sierra Leone, and she said, "Well, not now." Until I turned nineteen or twenty I needed to stay here and couldn't go back.

I said, "I don't like the winter. It's too cold." She said, "That's how it is in America." So it was kind of hard for me.

Plus, at school, there were some students who didn't like me.

There was this one girl who said she wanted to fight me. That was really challenging. I didn't fight her because I didn't have time for fighting. I didn't come to fight; I just came here to learn and make friends. Instead of fighting, I went to class and ate lunch with other kids. I ignored her.

I do track. That's my favorite sport. I used to do it when I was little in Sierra Leone, and I'm still doing it. The other thing that I did last year was student council. I was in the senate. I like to stay after school and hang out with friends. Sometimes I like to go out and get some food with my friends. For example, my school used to have a Chinese restaurant one block away, and I used to go there with friends whenever I had money. Well, my life now is kind of not going okay because me and my mom have some issues. Something happened, so now I live with my auntie, and it's not going great because she isn't at home. She goes to work, and we're still home by ourselves. We are hungry sometimes, so it's hard now.

I want to go back and live with my mom, but I have to wait. My hope for the future is to let the people who say I'm not going to end up going to college see me walking the stage and let them be proud of me. I want to take care of my little sisters when I grow up because I'm the oldest one. And to make my mom happy because she thinks that out of all her kids, I'm not the one who's going to end up going to college. I want to show her that I can do it and make her happy.

VIDEO LINKS

greencardvoices.org/speakers/nanah-jalloh

Quetzaltenango,
Guatemala

Willian Alonzo

From: Quetzaltenango, Guatemala
Current City: Minneapolis, MN

> "[WHEN I WAS IN GUATEMALA,] WE DIDN'T GO TO SCHOOL BECAUSE WE DIDN'T HAVE MONEY TO PAY FOR IT. . .SO I DECIDED TO COME HERE TO THE UNITED STATES TO FIND A BETTER LIFE FOR ALL MY FAMILY."

I was born in the city of Quetzaltenango, Guatemala. I lived in a small town—Cajola. I remember, when I was in Guatemala, I lived with all my family, but I had some problems. For example, we didn't have a lot of food, and my sister and my brothers didn't go to school because we didn't have money to pay for it. When I graduated from free public school, I stopped going to school because I had to pay for it. When I went to public middle school, I missed too many days because I had to work with my dad. Then I went to a school called Basico. I did not do many projects because the supplies were expensive and my family did not have money to buy them. In my free time I played soccer with my friends.

When I was in Cajola, some gangs tried to recruit me, but I did not want that. Then they tried to manipulate me. They said if I did not join them, other gangs would fight or kill me. So I decided to come here to the United States to find a better life for all my family.

One day, I took a bus from my city to the border of Guatemala and Mexico. I was there one night, and I found someone to help me to pass the border. We walked for like five hours in the mountains. I took many buses through Mexico, and also I took the train, the Beast. They called it the Beast because when immigrants are coming to the USA, they have to take this very dangerous train, and hundreds of people die because the extortionists would throw you off or shoot you. I was on the top of the train, and the sun was so hot, and in the rain I was wet.

I was on the train for five days. Then I took a car and someone helped me to get me to the border. I was at the border, in a house, for like one month. After that, someone took me to the mountains to wait.

Finally, I went to the border. It's like a river between the United States and Mexico. I was there for one week, with no food and no drinks. I ate leaves of trees every day. When I was there, I found someone to help me; it was like my guía to take me from Mexico to the United States. I walked many miles during the night. In the morning, the immigration was around me. The first time, I escaped. I walked alone for two days. It was the same thing—no food, no drinks.

I found a small town, and I found someone to help me. They were part of a gang, and they tried to give me drugs. They said the heroin would help me to not be scared. I did not take it because I didn't want to and because it could be addictive. I remember one day, before I left from Guatemala, I promised my mom I would never do drugs.

They contacted a woman to help me to bring me to my destiny, and she said okay. She took me, and she sent me to a city. In that city, the immigration took me, and they sent me to a center, or a jail. It was called the Cooler because it was so cold, and I had no sweater and no shoes. I was there like forty-eight hours. Finally, the immigration sent me to juvenile detention. I was there one month or two.

I have an uncle who lives in Minneapolis, Minnesota. He helped take me out of the center. He sent me to Wellstone High School. In school, I found a lawyer. She helped me to get a green card. Right now I have that green card, and I am here.

I live with my uncle; he's like my roommate. I send some money to my brothers because they are poor. They are going to school because I send money to them. I feel proud of myself. Also I support my family and send half the money for food and other things necessary for my family.

In the morning I go to school, and at night I'm working. Right now I have a job. I am a chef and the manager of my job. When I started that job, I was a dishwasher. I worked hard, step by step, to get that position.

I want to be an architect—an architect and a chef. My dream is that I can do them both. I'm looking for a scholarship to send me to Spain, because I want to be a good chef. I also want to be a motivational speaker.

greencardvoices.org/speakers/willian-alonzo

Mogadishu,
Somalia

Zamzam Shukri

From: Mogadishu, Somalia
Current City: Minneapolis, MN

"I SPOKE NO ENGLISH. SHE SPOKE NO ENGLISH. WE ONLY TALKED WITH OUR HANDS."

I'm from Somalia. I was born January 1, 1997. I came to Ethiopia when I was three years old. My mom was going to the United States. I went to a refugee camp with my dad and then my sister and brother. My grandmother came to Ethiopia. She died in Ethiopia. My sister was eleven.

Then I came to the United States—to Austin, Texas. I went to school for six months. I didn't know the bus stop, the country, or the people. The students spoke and I didn't understand. Then after one month, I knew the bus stop, and I had money for it.

In Austin, it was very difficult. I went to school, and one day, and then Wednesday and Friday, I didn't go. Then they called my father, asking, "Where is Zamzam?" It was difficult. I didn't understand all the teachers. I didn't understand the lunch. I felt bad because I didn't understand what the teachers said. One girl, Layla, was from Pakistan. Our hijabs were the same. Our lunch was the same. Our prayers were the same. I spoke no English. She spoke no English. We only talked with our hands. The girl from Pakistan has no phone, so today I cannot talk to her. In the future I will go to Texas and look for Layla.

Then I came to Minneapolis. My mom is here. I saw my mom. I go to school at Wellstone. I am happy—very, very happy. The Wellstone teachers are good, and the students are good. I am happy.

In my country, we go to school at 7:00 a.m. and then go to leave at 12:00 and go to lunch. In America, it's busy. 6:00 a.m. wake up, then at 7:30 a.m. I go to school. Then it is 6:00 p.m. It's very difficult because I am very busy with homework and the readings. If a student is absent, they'll call his mom.

I live here in Minneapolis. I live with my mom, sisters, and brothers. I go to school, and I work. I leave for work at 5:30 p.m. and finish at 9:30 p.m.

On the weekend, I go to the library, and then I come home, to my home community. I help my mom do the clothes washing, then at night I read a book. Every day I help my brother because his heart is sick. Every day I go to hospital with my brother and my mom. The doctor changes my brother's shirt because his hand is not working, and his hand is slow. My mother and I help my brother with the shirt. My brother has a wheelchair. He walks only a little bit. I feel sad because my brother is sick and broken and hurt. I help my mom every day.

In my future, I hope to finish high school. Then I'll finish college. Then I'll be a teacher. Then I'll go back to my country. My sister and my auntie and my cousin are still in my country. I miss you, my country.

VIDEO LINKS

greencardvoices.org/speakers/zamzam-shukri

Addis Ababa,
Ethiopia

Yonis Ahmed

From: Addis Ababa, Ethiopia
Current City: Minneapolis, MN

"WHEN I CAME TO THE AIRPORT, I DIDN'T KNOW HOW TO CHANGE TO ANOTHER PLANE. AND I DIDN'T KNOW HOW TO SPEAK ENGLISH. IT WAS DIFFERENT FOR ME."

I was born in Ethiopia, a country that has many different people. It's a big country. I lived with my brothers and my aunts in Ethiopia, and I also went to school. I walked to school. It was a big school. I liked to go to school. Everyone in my country spoke many languages, and I liked to know the languages they spoke. Every day after school I read books, and sometimes I played soccer on Saturday and Sunday. Sometimes I talked to my friends and said, "Guys, can you teach me your languages?" At that time my dad was living in Minneapolis, Minnesota, and my mom lived in Hargeisa, Somalia.

My mom is Somali, and my dad is Oromo. I have two parents. And I like my parents. They have different languages and are different people. I have two sisters and two brothers. They live in Ethiopia now. I am the youngest.

My dad has been in the United States for seventeen years, and he applied for a visa. My dad said, "I need my children to come to the United States." He did everything for the visa. The US Embassy said, "We will give you a visa tomorrow." Me and my brother came to the US Embassy in the morning, and then the US Embassy said, "We are sorry, and we can not give your brothers visas because they are older." They said only me because of my age. At that time, I didn't even feel happy. I said that if my brothers didn't get a visa, I didn't want a visa. I didn't even want to go to America. My brother said, "Don't worry. You have a chance. Get your visa and go. We will come one day, inshallah." I came

31

on March 5th, 2015.

I came by myself. The United States sent me the tickets on Qatar Airlines. First I went to Doha, and then I went to Chicago. When I came to America by myself, I went to Chicago first. My dad said my cousin was waiting at the airport in Chicago, but I did not see my cousin because the airport is very big. I showed the ticket to security, and he talked to me in English, but I did not understand very well.

I said, "Please, God, help me. This is my first time in America."

Then one manager came and said, "Show me your visa." My visa was in my bag, but my bag was in Minnesota. Some people said you get your bag in Minnesota. He said, "It is important to have a visa. If you don't have a visa, you . . . Look in the backpack and check if it is in your backpack." I went and looked. Finally I found my backpack and my visa! I showed him my visa, and he said, "Ok, you can go now," and he showed me the airplane going to Minnesota.

When I came to Minnesota, there was snow. I didn't see any snow in my country. The first time I saw snow, I thought it was salt. Minnesota is very cold, and when I came the first time, I was cold. Then I was just confused. I saw many people speaking a different language. When I came to the airport, I didn't know how to change to another plane, and I didn't know how to speak in English. That was different for me. It's so hard for me to speak in English.

When I came to Minnesota, my family was waiting at the airport, and they took me home. I have a family in Minnesota. I went to my cousin's house, my aunt's house. Auntie showed me everything. That was good for me. Then we went to the Mall of America. When I went to the Mall of America, that was a good plan, and the children were playing there, and I was having fun, laughing in there. I was just playing and having fun. When I came to the US, I thought all American people were very rich.

I love my life now. I go to school, to high school, and hope to finish school and go to college. My life is now good. I am happy. I made friends, and my parents are here. I go to school, and I play sometimes with my family and my friends. And now I learn everything about America—for example, job, school, and understanding people.

I hope, in the future, that my brothers will come the United States. And that I can finish high school and then college or university. And have a happy life.

VIDEO LINKS

greencardvoices.org/speakers/yonis-ahmed

San Pedro Sula,
Honduras

Jennifer Nuñez Paz

From: San Pedro Sula, Honduras
Current City: Minneapolis, MN

"WHEN MY MOTHER TOLD ME THAT WE BOTH WERE COMNING TO THE UNITED STATES, I GOT NERVOUS AND I THOUGH THAT MY LIFE WAS GOING TO CHANGE."

I am Jennifer, and I was born in San Pedro Sula, Honduras. I grew up with my grandparents, my older sister, and my cousins. My mom left me when I was six years old. We always had a dog and a rabbit at home. I loved the sea. We went there every weekend. I really miss my country, my community, my culture, the food. I miss all of my country.

When I was fourteen years old, my mom came back to Honduras to bring me to the United States. When my mother told me that we both were coming to the United States, I got nervous and I thought that my life was going to change. I felt kind of sad because I was leaving my grandparents and leaving my friends and cousins. We traveled through Honduras, Guatemala, Mexico, and Minnesota. To get into Guatemala, we took a car. It took us an hour. After that we got on the bus to go to Mexico, and then we traveled on the bus like for two hours. We crossed the river on a boat, and then we walked for less than ten minutes.

Coming to the United States, we were caught by the police. My mom and I and two little boys were all in jail for seven days. Finally, we got out of jail, and they gave us permission to be in the US. My mom and I went to court in that same year. We traveled by walking and in a bus, day and night. The journey was four days, and then we went to McCaulley, Texas. We were in immigration for six days. So the total days was eleven days. We traveled to Minnesota after.

At first it was difficult to be in the US, and I was depressed. After one week, I wanted to go back to Honduras. I missed all the food; the food had a different taste here. When I went to high school, I went to tenth grade. I felt alone and like a different person. I just always said "Yeah, yeah" because I didn't know the language, English. I took English in my country, but that was just one class.

Now I'm getting it. At Wellstone High School, the system is really good. I have translators and people who are helping me all the time, speaking Spanish, English, and a lot of languages. My life changed because finally I was living with my mother and my little sister. When I started to go to church with my family, I started to feel comfortable being here.

Now I love playing soccer. I go to church. I am learning English at church. There is a Latina church. They are always speaking Spanish and English. I learn a lot there. I am going to church every Sunday. Now I am part of the worship team at church. I love to go to the parks with my little sister. I love volleyball. I'm getting a job right now, and I think what I earn, and what my mom earns in a day, is a lot in my country. Five dollars is what you get in Honduras for one day. I think I love Minnesota. The weather is difficult and different obviously. Sometimes my stepdad asks me if I want to go back to Honduras. I say, "No, I don't want to go back right now."

At first I was interested in studying psychology, but I changed my mind. I want to study interior design, and I want to be a photographer, but I'm not sure. I want to have success in my life. I want to go to college and graduate. The education here in the US is different from Honduras. Here, there are a lot of opportunities to help students graduate from college.

Also my dream is to help my family. In the future I don't want to live here in Minnesota. I want to go back to Honduras and do what I want to. I wish to buy a lot of houses and land and also to have centers for people with needs.

VIDEO LINKS

greencardvoices.org/speakers/jennifer-nunez-paz

Mogadishu,
Somalia

Abdulahi Osman

From: Mogadishu, Somalia
Current City: Minneapolis, MN

> "FOR FIVE DAYS, I DID NOT GO OUTSIDE. I WAS IN THE HOUSE BECAUSE I DIDN'T KNOW HOW TO SPEAK IN ENGLISH MORE. I DIDN'T HAVE ANY FRIENDS, AND I DIDN'T KNOW ANYONE."

My name is Abdulahi. I was born in Somalia. I stayed there until I was seven. After that, I moved to Ethiopia. When we were in Africa, we didn't have a father. When I moved to Ethiopia, my mother and her mother came to Ethiopia also. It was safe there. That's why we went to Ethiopia. At that time, my mother's sister was in Sweden. She said, "Would you like to come to Sweden?" We said yes. After that, she tried to get us to Sweden. But we stayed in Ethiopia for five years. We applied and then appealed twice to go to Sweden, but they didn't approve us.

I remember I was afraid of gangs in Ethiopia. The first time when I saw them, I went out of my way to avoid them. Then my family said we would move to another village, and then we became neighbors of the gangs. I was afraid, but then we became friends.

My mother's friend said, "It's good to go to a refugee camp. Then you can go to America." That is why we went to refugee camp Sheder. We stayed in the refugee camp for four years. I started grade seven, and I finished grade seven, grade eight, and grade nine. When I was in Ethiopia, I learned English and Arabic and Amharic. I didn't go to school. My uncle taught me Arabic, English, Math, and Quran and also taught me how to read and write the Somali language.

One night I was outside when our caseworker in the refugee camp said, "Go inside your home now." I was not home, but my mother was home.

When we came back home, my mother said, "I have news to

help all of you."

And then we said, "Tell me, tell me."

"Shut your eyes." And then we made a circle. Then she said, "We're going America!"

And then, when I opened my eyes, I said, "Wow . . . no, impossible. Mom, is it true?"

"You know I am not telling a lie." Then we believed.

After that, my mom, three sisters, and one brother moved to America. We were six people if I add myself. When I came to America, I transferred to Chicago and then to Minnesota.

When I was in Chicago, in the airport, I needed the bathroom. I asked a policeman and then he said, "Come on." He said, "Sit here." I sat. Then he called IOM, my caseworker. He said, "He's lost, this man." And then I wondered what he meant when he said, "This man is lost."

After that, we moved to Minnesota. I've been here for two months and seven days. When I came to the airport, I met my aunt, her two daughters, and her husband. That night she said, "We'll go to my home." And we went to her home. For five days, I did not go outside. I was in the house because I didn't know how to speak in English more, I didn't have any friends, and I didn't know anyone. Then I got to this high school, Wellstone. My caseworker in Minnesota, Sir Jim he is called, I met at Wellstone. He is my only friend in Minnesota. I have only one friend.

Sometimes I am confused while taking the bus. When I was in Africa taking the bus, you'd say, "I need that stop; can you stop there?" But here you can't say that. Something that I like: when I was in Africa, I didn't know how to drive, but when I came here I learned.

It's different here. Me, I like soccer. When I was in Africa, I played soccer. When I came here, I played soccer in the grass. It's a beautiful place. In America, when someone kicks you, you don't feel bad. You are good here. No one plays with hands in America. That is different. But in Africa, when someone kicks you, you fall down. You bleed. You crash. It's bad. In Africa, they play with hands and hit you.

My mother, she's always saying, "Stop soccer, stop."

And I say okay. When she leaves home, I go play soccer. When she comes back, I stay home. Then she is happy for me and I am happy for her.

Here I'm new, but I look like a man who stayed here many years because, when I was in Africa, I learned English. I take English classes because I like to speak English. If I stay here one year or two years, my English will be better. I came to America to learn.

I don't miss Africa, but I miss friends. I think when I grow up I will miss Africa, but not now. I said, "We are going America." Then my friends said, "Oh good." Now in America, all night we talk in email. I miss them.

When I was in Ethiopia, my mother's brother had four brothers and three sisters. They all send money from abroad. There are eight of them, and they send money every month. They call every time and say, "Abdulahi, don't lie, don't have bad friends because if you lose your time . . ." and they are saying we need to become good people. When I am sleeping, I dream I am a doctor or an engineer. Because my family would like for me to have a good job and be a good man.

Why did I come to America? Because I want to succeed, and I want to get my dream, like being a computer engineer. I need to prove that dream for my family.

VIDEO LINKS

greencardvoices.org/speakers/abdulahi-osman

Cuenca, Ecuador

Nathaly Carchi

From: Cuenca, Ecuador
Current City: Minneapolis, MN

"I TRY HARD TO SHOW OTHER PEOPLE, TO SHOW THE BULLIES WHAT I CAN DO."

When we were in Ecuador, I lived with my mom. She was a single mom, and I remember that we had to pass through really hard times. We were really poor, and we didn't have a house to live in. We didn't have anything to eat. Sometimes, we had to live in the street. I remember those times. My mother left me when I was five years old. She came to America in order to give me a better life. After that, I lived with my godmother.

My godmother raised me. I say to her that she is my mother because she raised me, and also I lived with her for about eight years. She used to take care of me when I was one and a half years old.

Cuenca, my city, was peaceful. I remembered people selling things on the street. I liked to go to the corner of the parks to eat *chuzos,* which are grilled meats on a stick. I had memories about how my friends and I used to play basketball on Fridays. I always lost the games, but I loved how I spent time with my friends. My uniform of the school was really dirty. Every morning I loved to wake up and go to my godmother's restaurant to smell the aroma of *seco de pollo.* When I ate it, I felt confident with myself to go to school.

The system of education in Ecuador is different from the United States. I was in tenth grade of high school when I came. I felt that I was smart in my country because I learned everything in my native language.

One day I received a phone call from my mother. She told me

that I got the visa. I was really sad because I didn't want to leave my godmother, but also I was happy because I would see my mother again.

When I arrived to the United States and saw my mother, I felt really sad and bad because she was kind of a stranger to me. I didn't feel any love from her. It was really hard for me. Also people started to talk to me, and I couldn't understand anything. My first week, I went to Ramsey Middle School and it was really hard because the students started to bully me because I didn't speak English. People called me *burra*, *tonta*, all sorts of bad words. It was really hard for me.

I study hard, and now I am at Wellstone. I've started to speak more in English and write. I love to write in English, but I don't like to read. I try hard to show other people, to show the bullies what I can do.

When I came to the United States, I felt that I was not smart enough to learn the new language. Until now. I can speak English very well, but I am afraid of people laughing at me like the bullies did. When I came to the United States, my life got complicated, and I ended up losing my friends. Today I just have one friend, who showed me that I am important to her; we are still friends.

I'm a senior now. I want to graduate from high school and then go to college. I want to get a scholarship if I can, and if I can get a scholarship I want to go to the University of Minnesota. If I don't get the scholarship, I want to go to community college. I want to be an architect. I love math. I love to draw and design things.

VIDEO LINKS

greencardvoices.org/speakers/nathaly-carchi

Jijiga, Ethiopia

Kayd Falug

From: Jijiga, Ethiopia
Current City: Minneapolis, MN

"I WANT TO LIVE IN AMERICA FOR MANY YEARS. I WANT TO GO BACK TO ETHIOPIA ONE DAY BECAUSE I HAVEN'T FORGOTTEN WHERE I WAS BORN."

My life in Ethiopia was hard. If we needed to cook, we went outside because we didn't have a kitchen. I wasn't safe. That was hard for me. Ethiopian school is different. If you have money you can go to a good school with good subjects like geology and English. If you are a refugee, you go to bad schools. You don't learn English. The teachers are bad because they don't have money to teach the students. The students work hard, but the schools are bad. I did not learn English at this school. I wanted to go to a good school, but I didn't have money. I felt bad sometimes, but after three minutes I'd feel okay.

We left Ethiopia. My family and my cousins were eight people total. We lived in a refugee camp. I don't remember more.

First, I had to travel to a city in Ethiopia. Its name was Addis Ababa. Then I transferred to Germany. After, I came straight to New York. I slept one night in New York. Then I had to come straight to Minnesota.

When I first heard about going to America, I felt happy because I believed America was very good. I would have a lot of money. I would have to go to school. I would have safety. That's what I believed. So when I came America, some things I saw, and some things I didn't see. I didn't see the money. I didn't see free jobs. When we lived in Ethiopia, we believed in free jobs. You went to a job but got no money. I saw a lot of things.

I remember the first week. I was confused about the houses, I was confused about the streets, I was confused about the buses, I was confused about the snow . . . I was confused about many things because I never saw anything like them. It was confusing, but my family talked to each other. We said we never saw anything like this. They were confused. I slept for three days and woke on day four. At that time, I was not brave. The weather was like good weather. Then I learned everything.

My life now is good. I live with my mother, and I have two brothers. They live here. I have some cousins. I live some days with them, so my life now is good because I have money, I have school, and I have safety. It is good. Then I came to Wellstone. I have a weekend job. I work at Legendary Bakery. I make cake. I take my cousin's car. I work in the city Chaska. I like to play soccer. I like to watch TV and movies.

I want to live in America. I want to live in America for many years. I want to go back to Ethiopia one day because I haven't forgotten where I was born. I hope to be a company manager. I will be working and showing everyone what to do. Or I hope to be a driver on a city bus, because when I came here, I was confused by the buses. I want to do a hard job. I want to finish high school, I hope. Or I want to be a doctor. When I go back to Ethiopia, I will be a doctor. My life in America is good, plus I have a house with my family. That's what I have. So I have to go to school.

Kakuma, Kenya

Zamzam Ahmed

From: Kakuma, Kenya
Current City: Minneapolis, MN

"I WANT TO BE TEACHER IN MY FUTURE. I HOPE TO GO BACK TO MY COUNTRY, AND TO SEE MY COUSINS AND MY UNCLES."

My name is Zamzam. I was born in Kenya in 1998. I live with my parents and my uncles. I have six sisters and three brothers. My big sister is Sahra. She's nineteen years old. Second is Safiya; she's eighteen years old. I'm third—seventeen. My younger sister, Zaynab, is fifteen years old. Another, Zeytun, is twelve years old. The boys—Zakaria, he's ten years old and Said, he's eight years old. Nasra, she's six years old. Saleban is three years old.

When I lived in Kenya, I was a refugee. In Kenya, I went to school. We learned English and science and math and social studies. Then I moved to Kakuma when I was seven years old. Then, when I went to Kakuma, I lived there nine months. Sometimes in Kenya, me and my cousins would play games. We were so happy.

Then we moved to America in October, 2014. For two weeks, I didn't go to school. I didn't know how to speak in English. Then I felt a little bad. I remember one thing: I didn't know which was the bus stop for the school. I used my language, and I didn't know how to speak English. I just spoke a little English. When I first came to America, I felt a little excited, and now I feel so happy. Because now I've learned a little English and live with my family.

Now in America, I go to school—high school. I have friends. When I come to school, we have help to read the stories. With my brothers and my sisters, we go outside. We play and we come back home. Two days, Saturday and Sunday, we go to Dugsi Academy, and on Monday we go to school.

I hope to go back to my country and to see my cousins and my uncles. I miss my friends and my cousins. I want to be a teacher in my future. I really want to see my grandma and my uncles. Those are my hopes.

VIDEO LINKS

greencardvoices.org/speakers/zamzam-ahmed

Nairobi, Kenya

Yonis Yusuf

From: Nairobi, Kenya
Current City: Minneapolis, MN

"I WAS SO EXCITED BECAUSE PEOPLE SAID TO ME THAT I WOULD SEE MONEY ON THE STREETS. BUT WHEN I CAME, I DID NOT SEE ANYTHING LIKE MONEY."

I was born in Kenya, in a place called Nairobi, in 1997. My family came from Somalia because there was a war going on. For six years, we were in the middle of Kenya and Somalia. The people in Kenya decided they did not want Somalis in Kenya. The United States government decided to give us a place—Nakuru, for Somalis in Kenya. The Kenyans were happy we had a place because they didn't want us in Kenya, but we had one place for us to go. The day we came to Nairobi and went to Nakuru, the US government said we had a place with rice and food. They gave us all an interview. We stayed in Nakuru for seven years. Eventually I went to school in Nakuru, but I did not go to school in Nairobi. We did not have more water. We only had a little rice and sugar, and they gave us maize.

In 2002, I went to visit Somalia. I got to visit with my mom and my family. I stayed three months, and then I came back to Kenya. I was living with my auntie. It was in 2006 that my grandfather was killed. He was killed by Al-Shaabab.

Our country, Somalia, was really bad with fighting troubles, so the United States helped us as a refugee community. So I came to America.

It was in 2011 when we came to America. I was so excited because people said to me that I would see money on the streets. But when I came, I did not see anything like money. I was so happy that I was going. We went to Dubai for eight hours and then Belgium. Then

I was in New Jersey for four hours, and then I went to Chicago for ten hours, and I came to Minneapolis at midnight. I was with my aunt.

The first time in the United States it was so difficult, with the people speaking English and many things being different. I came with my auntie. We came in summertime. School wasn't for two months or three months. It was time for the school to end when I came, but I came to school as a freshman in August. I was trying to tell everyone I was not a freshman. I finished many classes in Kenya.

My life is so difficult with the life in Kenya and the life right now in the United States. So difficult. Because in Kenya, we were living as refugees, and the United States helped us and gave us a little bit of money. I wasn't sure about the new life, but they gave us a car, one thousand dollars, and we could buy anything that we wanted, so that was different. Before coming to America, my auntie and uncle gave me $2,000, like food stamps. I was so happy. In Kenya we had little food, and here I had the food stamps for more food.

Now I play basketball at Franklin Ave. and Chicago Ave. in the summertime. In the winter I play in the gymnasium. I really like my sports. I like basketball. I really want to finish high school and college and become a mechanic. That is my legacy in life. I want to have a better life in the future. I want to stay in the United States. I am happy to be here forever and visit my country.

greencardvoices.org/speakers/yonis-yusuf

Douala, Cameroon

Dorette Nguelefack

From: Douala, Cameroon
Current City: Minneapolis, MN

"AFTER SCHOOL, I GO TO THE LIBRARY. I LEARN MORE ABOUT ENGLISH. I LEARN MORE ABOUT AMERICA, AND I CAN LEARN MORE ABOUT THE WORLD."

My life in Cameroon was very simple. I lived in Cameroon, in the city of Douala. Douala is the capital economy of Cameroon because a lot of people send merchandise. I lived with my family, my father and my mother. I have two brothers and two sisters. I'm the second child of my parents. They live together in the same home. My mom is a pastor and my father is an engineer mechanic. I went to school Monday through Saturday, 6:00 a.m. to 5:00 p.m. It was not easy. I walked twenty minutes to school every day. After school I went to the library and read books because I like reading books. I read French books because I spoke French only.

It was not easy because sometimes I went to school and sometimes I did not go to school because of money. The school is very expensive in Cameroon. I went to church in my free time. In America, the parents care if you have a problem. The parents support you. In my country, Cameroon, parents don't support you if you have a problem. People don't care about the rights of children. In my country, I worked and I supported myself. I wanted to go to school. It was very hard for me. This was my life in my country.

I came to America on January 27th, 2015. I have spent one year in this country, this new country. When I was two or three years old, my auntie wanted to bring me to this country. She had spent twenty-five years in America. My auntie said she did not want me to live in poverty. She wants all my family to live together. She tried to get a visa for my family for sixteen years. When she said there was a visa, I came. I came here to this country with all my family together, at the same time.

It was very hard at first because I didn't speak English. But at the same time, I knew that I wanted to accomplish my dream in this country. I 100% had to accomplish my dream in this country.

The first day when I came to America, the first hard thing was language because I didn't know English. The second was that I saw that the people were different in this country. It wasn't the same education as my country or the same life as my country.

I remember, coming to America at first, the roads were very different. Everything was clean and all was orderly. People respected the traffic laws. I think that is good because everybody in this country works a lot, so that is respectful. It was very different. It is not like my country. It is beautiful. I see all that in the movies.

The country of America is a country for immigrants. I see different people that I never saw in all my life. I see education. Education is good. I realize America is a country to help me realize my dream better than my country. In this country, I want to learn about more things in the world and about the world.

The food is not very natural here. It's manufactured and fat. The chicken is too fat. To eat good food, you have to have money in this country. But at the same time, I like American food!

When I came, I couldn't believe my heart. It was my first winter. The winter is good. "God," I said to my mother, "if we had winter in our country, people would die. People don't have money in our country." But here I say, "If God makes winter, people can protect themselves, buy clothes, and have a car that they can drive because in winter it's difficult to drive." God didn't put winter in my country because people will want to die.

My life now is good because now I can speak English. Every day, Monday through Friday, I go to MCTC first. After, I go to Wellstone International High School, and I have more experience about life and about the world. I didn't believe high school is free here. You have all the support from the teachers. People care about your education. Oh my God I feel happy. I have everything to accomplish my dream in this country.

I live with my auntie, together with my father and my mother. On the weekend I work. I'm a cashier at a store. I work, and it is great because they pay me. I could work in my country, but the boss wouldn't pay me. Here I work twelve hours a week. After school, I go to the library. I learn more about English, I learn more about America, and I learn more about the world.

In my country, Cameroon, I had an accident. I was sixteen years old. I didn't go to school, I stayed in the home, and I went to the hospital. It made me sad. I said, "When I graduate, I want to be a nurse because if the people taking care of me felt good . . ." I like helping take care of people. I want to graduate this year. First, I want to have my nursing degree, then I want to go to a four-year medical school. After that I want to be a surgeon. St. Cloud University already admitted me. I want to apply to other colleges too.

I can remember nineteen years of my life in my country. I cried everyday because it was not easy, because I didn't get to accomplish my dream. It was very difficult to live in my country. Sometimes there was poverty. In my country, people don't care about women. They don't care if you want to go to school. But I say, "I am a woman. God didn't create me like a man. I want a good education."

I believed and I believed and I believed that one day I would have a visa for this country, and one day, by the grace of God, I had a visa. My life changed, and now I want to have an impact with my life. I want to impact the world of many people. I know by my work I can have an impact on people. I want to thank God because now in this country I have more chances to accomplish my dream. This country is all for me. All that I need is to have a good education. I want to be a good patriot. I want to help people, take care of people. I don't care about the time. I don't care about temptation. I want to accomplish my dreams. I know everything in this country is possible if you work hard and if you have a vision. And if you know who you are. I know who I am.

When I came to this country, I saw they have heaven and they have the hell. But you can choose heaven, every day of your life, by the actions you take in your community. You are free to choose something you want to be. I choose to be a part of heaven by my actions and by my work. I know who I am. I know that people in the world need my knowledge. People of the world need the things I have in my mind. I try to do what I can to make an impact.

And one thing I want to add: I want to thank this country for everything and for making my life better.

VIDEO LINKS

greencardvoices.org/speakers/dorette-nguelefack

Kebri Beyah,
Ethiopia

Khadar Muhumed

From: Kebri Beyah, Ethiopia
Current City: Minneapolis, MN

"RIGHT NOW MY LIFE'S BETTER. . .I KNOW A LITTLE MORE ENGLISH. SO I CAN GO ANYWHERE."

My name's Khadar. My parents are from Somalia, but they lived in Ethiopia, so I was born in Ethiopia. I began in the elementary school and went there until high school, so I have lot of friends there. Me and my friends, we grew up there in Ethiopia. I lived for eighteen years in Ethiopia. I lived with my mom, my father, and siblings. I lived with other family members too, like my uncle.

We were refugees in Ethiopia, so we began in this program in 2006 to move to America. Somalia doesn't have any peace; it's war. So we began in 2006, and in 2014 I came to the United States. We waited a long time to go to the US. We waited eight years.

June 6th, 2014, was the day that we came to the United States. I remember that day. I remember my family, my dad and my mom, saying we're moving to the United States. Everybody began to get ready, to move there. We bought new clothes. I said, "Bye, I am moving to the United States," to my friends. A lot of friends were sad. Me too—I was crying. It was sad because we grew up together. I knew them and they knew me.

The first day I came to America, everybody was excited—me and my family. We were scared. When we came to the airport, nobody knew English. No one knew where we were. So everybody was scared, saying, "Oh, look at this. What is this? Where are we?" Everybody was crying and scared. Me too, actually. Me too.

First we went to New York. After New York, we went to North Carolina, to the town of Greensboro. We were there for fifteen days.

Fifteen days, my family and I were inside the home, nobody going outside. We looked out the window; we saw people walking outside. My dad and my mom were scared. We didn't know any English or anything in America. My cousin's family lived in Minnesota, so they called my family. They said to move to Minnesota. A lot of my friends, a lot of people from Somalia, they were here. That's why we moved to Minnesota.

When I came here to Minnesota, I went to the twenty-four-hour Somali mall. There were a lot of Somali. When I see a lot of Somali, I am happy. I used the Somali language, and I felt happy. It was like a little Somalia.

One day, I was walking and I saw there were some homeless guys. Me, I didn't know any English, and I used only one word in English. That word was "yes." Everybody was talking to me, and I answered, "Yes, yes, mister, yes." That's the word I knew. The homeless, they were asking me, "Oh hi, bro, you have a quarter?"

"Yes," I said.

So the guys said, "Give it to me . . ."

My cousin was with me, and he translated and said, "Give it to him."

"What am I to give him?" I said, "You have money?"

"No, no, bro, it's America, I don't have money!" So this guy was homeless, and he didn't have work, and he didn't have a home. That's why he asked for the quarter.

So I said, "Oh my God, America!" So that's happening in Minnesota.

Right now I live with my auntie and cousins and family. My family lives in Willmar; me, I'm here in Minneapolis, Minnesota. Right now my life's better. I go to school. I go to the library. I play soccer. I know a little more English, so I can go anywhere. I visit my family in Willmar. I have a great time.

Willmar is my little town. My friend is there, and my family's there. Willmar has a lake and a downtown Somali mall. When I go, I have lots of fun.

For the future—actually, I don't know—but sometimes I want to be a police officer or counselor. But I don't know what I will be.

I always want to do something good. I like education; I do a lot of education, so maybe I will go to college or university. That's what I want to share with other people: Don't lose your time. Don't waste your time. You have to go to high school, then to college, and then become whatever you want to be. You should have education. You can be whatever you want.

VIDEO LINKS

greencardvoices.org/speakers/khadar-muhumed

Cuenca, Ecuador

Jennifer Erraez

From: Cuenca, Ecuador
Current City: Minneapolis, MN

> "IT'S SO DIFFICULT HERE. SOMETIMES IT'S SO COLD; SOMETIMES IT'S SO HOT. BUT I'M HERE. I'M STILL HERE."

My life in Cuenca, Ecuador, was so awesome. I had many friends. My friends loved me and my family. My friends helped me all the time. My life in Cuenca, Ecuador, was very full. I had a lot of family. My family went to parties all the time, national parties, and participated and danced. I was so happy in my country.

I remember when my father and my mom said, "Today, you go to the United States."

"What? Why?"

She said, "It's time to go."

The day we came here to the United States was the birthday of my sister, my younger sister, and my family was so sad. I was also sad when we came because I had my cousin; he loved me, and I loved him. At that moment, I thought it was bad. I didn't want that.

The first month, and first week, I remember I didn't like it because I didn't understand the language. Some people could speak in Spanish, but when you're speaking Spanish, they say, "What?! What are you talking about? What, you don't understand me?"

"No, I don't speak English!" Whoa. It was so difficult. But I learned. I understand now—a little bit, but I understand.

When coming to the United States, my first school was Edison. But I had problems last year, the first semester. I had problems with the father of my baby. I changed to Wellstone for the next semester, the second semester. I like Wellstone. Some people are Spanish and some are Somali, but the people are so friendly. I like it, but I love my country. It's difficult, and I'm missing everything in my country. I don't like it here because sometimes it's so cold and sometimes it's so hot. But I'm here. I'm still here

My goal is to graduate and then go to college. I want to go to work. My baby is five months old. My baby's name is Adriana. For my baby, I want the best for her. That is my idea and my decision. For her, everything is for her right now.

VIDEO LINKS

greencardvoices.org/speakers/jennifer-erraez

Mogadishu,
Somalia

Abdinasir Hussein

From: Mogadishu, Somalia
Current City: Minneapolis, MN

> "I WAS CONFUSED ABOUT THE TALL BUILDINGS. I DIDN'T KNOW HOW TO DRIVE A CAR, AND I DIDN'T KNOW HOW TO TAKE THE BUS. I WAS CONFUSED MOST DAYS. THEN I ADAPTED."

I was born in Somalia in 1996. Everyone knows Somalia's fighting in the wars of two groups. I decided to leave for another country. I was five years old. I don't remember much. I lived with my grandmother. She is a good person. I never forgot my grandmother. I love her. I left Somalia and I came to Kenya in 2008. Until 2013, I lived in Kenya. In Kenya, I went to school and work. I got married in Kenya, and I have one daughter. We are divorced now. Then my mom decided for us to leave Kenya and come to the United States. When I left Kenya, I was so sad because I left my friends. Sometimes they call me.

I said goodbye to all my friends, my daughter, and my ex-wife. I miss my girls right now. I feel for them. All my friends feel sad, and my baby is crying, and tears come to my eyes. I feel bad. I never forgot all my friends; they love me.

I flew to Minneapolis. I transferred in London and then to the United States, and then I stayed in Minneapolis. My mom was waiting at the airport, and my uncle, and my auntie, all of my relatives were waiting for me. Everybody hugged me because they missed me. I had not seen them for a long time. Right now, I live with my mom and my stepfather. By this time, I missed my daughter. Every other night I talk to my lovely daughter. The one I love is my daughter.

My mom had been living for twenty years already in the United States. I like my mom. She sent a visa for me, and I came to the United States. She helps me every day. My mom lives with my stepfather.

Every day I think about how to get happy. So I like to help my mother. I love my mother. She took care of me when I was young. I like all my relatives. Some of my relatives live in the United States of America; some of my relatives live in Somalia. All that I say is that I appreciate my mom and my other relatives.

When I first arrived, I was confused about the tall buildings. I didn't know how to drive a car, and I didn't know how to take the bus. Or how to take the train. I was confused most days. Then I adapted. And I had to take the bus.

My life right now is good. It's very, very good because I drive a car, I go to school, and I work. My job is good. I work for a postal office. I can graduate in May. When I graduate, I will go to college. That's what I think. I want to be a good man. I wish to complete university, maybe in computer science. I want to be a manager and leader. I like my life to be at a high level. I would love to have a new marriage and a house. I would like a big life for myself. Actually, I live for my daughter. I miss my daughter. I like to tell everybody I know that I wish to go back to my home to see my young kid. I want to keep and take care of her.

VIDEO LINKS

greencardvoices.com/speakers/abdinasir-hussein

Kakuma, Kenya

Safiya Ahmed

From: Kakuma, Kenya
Current City: Minneapolis, MN

> "I'M HAPPY BECAUSE I LIVE WITH MY FAMILY—ALL MY SISTERS. ALL MY BROTHERS. THAT IS GOOD. I HOPE I HAVE A GOOD LIFE WHEN I FINISH HIGH SCHOOL AND BECOME A DOCTOR."

My name's Safiya. I lived in Kenya. I was a refugee in Kenya. All of my family members were refugees. I came to the United States as a refugee. I loved living in Kenya. Sometimes we went to the school. It was not a good school. After, I moved to Kakuma, a refugee camp; that's the same for all refugees. In Kenya, I played with my friends. We ran in the street. I remember saying, "I'm first! I'm first!" We were running and saying that. I was so happy. All my family went to the USA.

First, when I came to America, I was afraid because I saw many different people. I got lost in the airport. I lived in Atlanta, Georgia for three weeks. I was saying, "Where is my house?" I saw many people speaking a language, but it was different. I knew one language in Somalia, and I didn't speak English. After I moved to Minneapolis, I saw my cousin. I was happy because many Somali are here in Minneapolis, Minnesota. That's good. I am happy.

I live with my family. I go to a new school in America. I feel happy. I can speak a little English right now. I think I came to a good place because I was seeing good friends, a good school, and good teachers.

Minneapolis and Atlanta, Georgia are very, very different places. When I went to Atlanta, Georgia, I did not have any cousins. All of my cousins are here in Minneapolis. When I was coming to Atlanta I felt very confused because I didn't have school or any people I knew. I didn't know how to ride the bus or go to the market. In Atlanta, I didn't see many Somalis. I only saw American people.

When I was in Africa, I thought America had a lot of money. When I came, I didn't see money. The people said, "If you want money, you get a job!"

I said, "You have a job?" After that, I didn't see money. I went to school.

When I was in my country, I didn't know how to play soccer. But when I came to the United States, I learned how to play soccer. I played on the Wellstone High School soccer team. I have a new school and all my friends here. I have many friends here America. I am happy because I live with my family—all my sister, all my brothers. That is good.

I dream that I will finish high school and I go to college or university. I hope I will return to my country because I miss my country. I miss my little cousin. I hope to be a doctor. I don't want to forget my country. I hope I have children. I hope to have a lot of money here.

VIDEO LINKS

greencardvoices.org/speakers/safiya-ahmed

Gondar, Ethiopia

Aksum & Tsion Woldeyes

From: Gondar, Ethiopia
Current City: Minneapolis, MN

"SHE HAS ME AND I HAVE HER. SHE IS MY FRIEND AND I AM HER FRIEND."

Aksum Woldeyes: We were born in Ethiopia in the city of Gondar. We grew up in a small town called Kola Diba. We lived with our mother in Ethiopia before we came here to the United States. We have four sisters and five brothers.

Tsion Woldeyes: We went to school in Ethiopia until eighth grade. We had lots of friends in our neighborhood and at school too. At school we had eight friends, and in the neighborhood we had three friends and two best friends. Our life was great. We spent time with them and we played. We had a time set up to play and to study with them. We really had a good time there in Ethiopia.

AW: When we were little, our dad came to Kenya because of his sister and a civil war. After that, he went to Minneapolis.

TW: Our father started the process to get the visa for the nine of us. But eventually, our two sisters got the first visa. They came here, and after two years, he sent a visa for three of us—for my older brother and the two of us. We went to the capital city of Ethiopia; it's called Addis Ababa. We went there for two months to process our visa.

Our older brother finished our process, and he told us, "We're gonna go to America."

We were like, "What?" We were in Addis Ababa for two months, but we didn't say goodbye to our friends or family . . . We didn't say goodbye to our mother or our little brother. We were sad, and we didn't even know what we were going to get in America. Then they told us that our sisters and our father and friends were there, and they told us we would go to school, a better school, and we would have friends.

AW: We weren't happy. We were sad because we didn't say goodbye to our mother, brothers, and relatives. But we were a little happy because we would get to see our sisters and father. When we arrived, there were lots of people with them, and they spoke Amharic. The first time it wasn't like . . . happy . . . or something. We didn't know how to speak English.

First we went to Wellstone High School. It was the first day for us, and we were like, "Oh my God . . ." It was sad because we didn't understand what they said. The English was hard for us. The teacher at Wellstone helped us with English. She gave us books, and she helped us with everything, and then it became better.

AW: For the winter, we were about to cry because it was cold. In Ethiopia, the weather is good. It's not cold, it's not hot—it's in the middle. Here, it changes. When it's summer, it's hot. It's better when it's fall and spring. But winter—it's so cold. We didn't know there was snow. Our father told us that it wasn't that cold when we came here first, but after that, it was cold, really.

For the first two months, we didn't actually go outside by ourselves because we didn't know the place, and our dad thought that we would be lost if we went by ourselves. Even if we wanted to make friends, we couldn't make one because of a lack of communication and a lack of English language.

Now in Minnesota, we've learned to speak English and we've learned to communicate well with others. In school, we have lots of friends who are from different countries. Being at Wellstone International High School taught us how to work in a diverse place and to help each other.

TW: Our hobbies now: We like to go to the library, check out books, and read. Sometimes we use the computer there. We really like to spend our time with our friends. But as you know, American people are really busy, so . . . she has me and I have her! She is my friend, and I am her friend.

We take classes at MCTC. So when we first started at MCTC, it was really hard because we didn't really know how to speak English or write and use grammar correctly. It was really hard, but now we are getting it, and it's not that hard right now.

AW: We have an Upward Bound Vision Quest program. In the summer, they take us to visit a college and then stay there for six weeks. It's fun, really fun. They pay us money for a week, and then if you want a job, you can get one there. It's a STEP-UP job.

AW: Our mother came here with our two brothers in 2015, about eight months ago. So we are happy here now because we got our mother, father, sisters—all except two brothers. The oldest is in Ethiopia.

TW: But our mother is not happy here in America. She wants to go back because here we pay rent every month, and my dad said we have to pay for rent—her, my sister, and I. We live in a different house because my father and mother live in public housing, so they cannot live with us. They said we have to pay rent for both of our houses. My mom said, "Oh my God, why am I here. We're paying rent every month. In our country in Ethiopia, we have two houses in a village." My mom used to rent out the house and get paid for it. She said, "Oh my, this is the opposite that I get here!" So she wants to go back.

AW: And her mother, our grandmother, is old, and she's in Ethiopia. So she said, "I have to see her."

TW: We want to study in medical technology or be pharmacists. After we finish college or university, I want to go back to Ethiopia and work there. My family, my relatives, my cousins, are there. We don't have any cousins in Minneapolis. I want to go back. I don't know about her.

AW: Yes, me too. I want to go back and work there, in a hospital. There are a lot of people who are sick in our country, so I want to help them. I want to go to university and become a pharmacist. I want to become a pharmacist to provide safe medicine for people who are sick—at the right time. I want to be with my family, and my cousins, all the people that are there in Ethiopia. My father's sister, brother, everyone is there.

TW: Many people in this country think every person in Ethiopia immigrated to this country because Ethiopia is poor. But I don't think that's the reason that we immigrated here. Ethiopia was poor a long, long, long time ago, but now we're not that poor. They think we immigrated because we cannot work there. But we immigrated to find our family and live with them. Lots of people immigrated because of their families, not because our country is poor. That's what I want to add.

VIDEO LINKS

greencardvoices.org/speakers/aksum-tsion-woldeyes

Fuzhou, China

Quan Guan

From: Fuzhou, China
Current City: Minneapolis, MN

"I WANT TO BE AN ENGINEER IN THE FUTURE. I CAN CREATE SOME NICE BUILDINGS AND USEFUL MACHINES FOR PEOPLE TO USE."

My life in China was good. I lived with my aunt, and I went to school Monday to Friday. I lived at school because my home was far from school. The Chinese education is very hard. I had to wake up early and go to bed late. After class, I liked to play soccer. I had lot of friends in China.

In China, I had to learn about nine subjects. It was very hard. I had to wake up at 6:00 a.m. and go to my home at 10:00 p.m. I had to use about five hours to finish my homework per day. I couldn't get enough sleep Monday to Friday, so Sunday and Friday were a good chance for me to sleep.

I moved to the United States because my parents lived there. I missed them so much. Also, in the United States I can get a good education, and the air in the United States is very fresh. Also, in the US, how successful you are depends on how hard you work.

I came to America in November, 2014. That day, it was raining, but I still felt very excited and happy because I could see my parents again. When I saw my mother, she recognized me immediately. Then she gave me a hug and held me tight. Meanwhile, I saw a tear shining in her eyes, and it was almost out of her eyes.

Also, I was excited to know about the Americans and to begin my new life. However, the first week was very hard because the environment in America is very different from China. It's very dry and cold. In addition, I felt very sleepy all day in the first week. It was very hard.

After a week, I got to Minnesota. Then I was in shock because I couldn't speak and understand English even though I had studied English in China for four years. Four years of hard work—just like a bubble, it was gone. Because I am a shy and quiet person, I got in trouble for not communicating with my teacher and classmates. It was getting better when I took a class at MCTC.

Now I'm a student at Wellstone International High School, and I go to MCTC for English class in the morning. In the weekends I do some drawing and origami. I like biking during the summer.

I want to be an engineer in the future. I can create some nice buildings and useful machines for people to use. For sure, the first step to being an engineer is to study hard in college. My grandma always told me on the phone, "You should go to the college in the US because it is better than Chinese college." Therefore, I will study hard and show my family how useful of a person I am.

VIDEO LINKS

greencardvoices.org/speakers/quan-guan

Liboi, Somalia

Abdirahman Hirad

From: Liboi, Somalia
Current City: Minneapolis, MN

"THIS IS THE COUNTRY THAT GAVE ME THE OPPORTUNITY TO LIVE, SO I JUST WANT TO PAY THEM BACK AND HELP OTHER PEOPLE THAT ALSO HAVE DIFFICULT TIMES."

Well first of all, my name is Abdirahman. I was born in Liboi. That's a small place in Southern Somalia. I went to elementary school there for my first four years. I lived with my mom and my father, but my mom left us when I was six years old. There were four siblings—all boys. Two girl cousins lived with us. I did go to school, but there was war, and it was difficult in those circumstances. I played soccer sometimes with my friends during the afternoons. In Somalia, my dad was a doctor. He graduated from medical school in Russia and had a small private clinic in town. My mom was a housewife.

My mom left me in 2005. I hardly remember that time because I was so young. She had to move to Kenya, a border country, to the city Nairobi. The last time that I saw her she said to me, "We may never meet again," because she was looking for a new life in a country that was so far away, thousands of miles away, which was the United States.

She went to a refugee camp in the southern part of Kenya. She lived there for a couple of years while the hard process was taking place. Finally, in December 2006, she was able to come here to the United States.

The moment before she went to the United States, she phoned us, all the family, and said, "Well, this is the last time that I will be here, because we may never see each other again."

So I said, "I wish you good luck. We may meet again." Then, finally, we met again in ten years' time.

I really missed her a lot because the family split up. You know, you can understand, when the family splits up, there are problems that they face. I was really missing my mom because she was the kind of person that was so helpful to us.

Later I moved to Kenya because of the war that was taking place in Somalia. Liboi was a strategic place, as it was on the way between Kenya and Somalia. The rebels and the government collided so many times in order to control the town.

So we moved to Nairobi. I continued my primary education there, which was grades four to eight. I continued right there up to high school, and then after that I came here to Minnesota. In Somalia, I took some English classes, but when I moved to Kenya, I struggled to adopt the new language, which was Kiswahili.

A year before I moved to the US, my father died of a stroke. It was very challenging because he took care of me until I was seventeen. We lived in the same room, slept in the same room, and ate dinner together every day. I was very sad, and it was very difficult. My mother, who, in the meantime, moved to the US, sent us a visa, and we moved to the US a year after my father passed. I came with my three brothers, but my two cousins had to stay because they did a DNA test. The DNA test only proves who is mother and child so they couldn't pass the DNA test. They don't have any family in Kenya, and I miss them. I was especially close to my cousin, who lived with us for almost our entire life. That is the person I really miss.

I remember when I found out about my visa. Last January, almost a year ago, the embassy of the United States in Kenya called us and said, "Wow, you are ready. Your visa's ready. You can book your ticket whatever time you want," and then I was ecstatic. I was so delighted. It was a dream come true, a dream I was dreaming for so long, to come to a great country, the United States, and to build my career—in terms of my education, and my country, my family, my future. It was an incredible moment at that time, really. I can't even describe the feeling that I had at that moment. It was an amazing feeling.

In terms of the journey to the US, it was too long a journey. I've never been through a journey like that. It was almost an entire day and night, twenty-four hour journey. Finally, we arrived in the Minneapolis airport after a long, long journey. And then finally I was reunited with my mom, which was an absolutely incredible moment at that time. When I had last seen my mom, I was six, and when I saw her next I was eighteen. She looked different.

When I first started living with my mother, it was incredible. Because I'd never been with my mom, and then to live again with her, it was an amazing moment. Living with your mom after so many years of missing her is something that you can't describe in a sentence. It was unbelievable. I thank God for making me live with my mom again. It was a wonderful moment really to live again with my mom.

When I first got to America on January 21st, it was night. And at that time, it was winter. I had never experienced winter because in Africa there's no winter. The weather's so constant all the time, every month. Then I came here . . . it was so cold. The temperature was so freezing; it was minus at that time. I said, "Wow, what's going on here?" I never expected the weather to be as harsh as that. I miss the weather in Africa. It was constant, and you saw the sun all the time.

I thought everyone lived comfortably here in America, but when I came here I quickly realized you have to work hard. The third day after arriving, I was in the car with my mom, shopping, and I saw a man on the corner of the street holding a cardboard sign stating he was homeless. It was so cold, so harsh. Then my mom told me there are many people that are homeless in America. I couldn't believe it!

If I compare the life in Somalia and in Kenya, it's totally different. There is a war that has been going on in Somalia since 1991 and is still going on right now. But in Kenya, it's a peaceful country that is stabilized and has never experienced any war. You cannot compare these two nations.

In terms of general life, there are some similarities that they have. In both of them the education is so expensive. For example, in elementary and high school, both Somalia and Kenya are so expensive that most of the parents cannot afford to pay for their children's school fees. School from grades one to eight is free; that was good, but after that it was very expensive. Which lead so many students, some of my friends even, to drop out of school. In the United States, high school—it's so free, everything's so free, even the lunch is free. But in Kenya and Somalia, most of the African countries, it's not like that. It's totally different.

My life now, it's just a normal life that a person lives. My mom, myself, and my other brother live in one building. I'm enjoying the life in Minneapolis. I'm adapting to the new system of this new country. My favorite sport in the US is WWE wrestling. I watch a lot of that. It's kind of my hobby. I even watched it yesterday for four hours. I like soccer too. Sometimes I miss the fresh food in Africa. Here you go to the refrigerator, and the food is two or three days old.

I'm graduating this June. I applied to the University of Minnesota, Duluth. You have to go there if you want to be a doctor. I am waiting to hear about a scholarship.

My future hope is to become a doctor, especially a children's doctor. That's something that I'm dreaming of because my father was a doctor as well. I just want to follow in his footsteps. When I become a doctor, I just want to help the patients. I just want to help communities. I just want to be part of building strong communities in the United States because the United States is the first country to bring communities closer, helping communities, needy people, and people who are poor. That's what I want to accomplish and that's what I want to pay back to this country. This is the country that gave me the opportunity to live, so I just want to pay them back and help other people that also have difficult times.

greencardvoices.org/speakers/abdirahman-hirad

Guayaquil, Ecuador

Alexandra Irrazabal

From: Guayaquil, Ecuador
Current City: Minneapolis, MN

> "WHEN I WAS IN THE AIRPLANE, I WAS THINKING, HOW IS MY MOM GOING TO LOOK RIGHT NOW? I DIDN'T KNOW HER, AND SHE DIDN'T KNOW ME."

I was born in Ecuador, a place that's called Guayaquil, but most of the time I lived in La Troncal. That's a little place. I was living with my grandma. I helped my grandma at home. She worked a lot. In Ecuador, you have to work the whole day just for ten dollars. That's really hard. I went to school when I was five years old. My favorite class was science. On Sundays, I hung out with friends and went to a place with pools. Every day, after 5:00 p.m., the kids went out to play games.

My mom went to Spain when I was two years old because we didn't have enough money. My grandma told me that my mother told me that, but I was very little. She said she was going to leave the country because she needed money for the things that I needed. She left, and I was very sad. She called me and told me that she found a job. She sent money for us, and I went to school and bought my own things and helped my mom with the food for us. She left for two years, and she got back when I was four. She stayed with me until I was seven years old. When she was there, she was working hard. Then, when I was seven years old, she told me she was going to leave again. I was mad at her because she was going to leave me again, and I didn't like that. I was very sad.

I remember my grandma telling me that my mom was calling. I got on the phone, and she just was talking to me, saying that she had papers so I could have a visa and come to be with her. I was very excited. I was like, "Yeah, I'm gonna go to America. That's gonna be fine."

But I was sad too because I was going to leave my grandma alone. We just lived together—her and me. When she told me that I was going to come in a few months, I was very happy because I would know my brother. I didn't know my brother; I just saw pictures. When she told me that, I was so excited, and she asked me if I wanted to come, and I said yes. But I was also very sad, thinking about all my friends I would not see anymore. Also, I cried because I was going to leave my grandma alone.

When I was in the airplane, I was thinking, "How is my mom going to look right now? How is my brother gonna be?" When I was already in Minneapolis, I called her with a phone from the guys at the airline. I called her, and she told me, "Yeah, I'm gonna be there in a few minutes. I'm downstairs." When she came, I didn't know her, and she didn't know me. I look very different in pictures—that's what she told me. When I saw her, she was searching for me. She told a girl that was in the airport to call me on the microphone. I knew that was my mom. I just ran and hugged her, and I was crying, because I was so excited. Downstairs were my brother and my uncle. And yeah, she was there, and I was really happy. The day was August 24, 2011.

The first week in America, it was so bad. When I got home, after they picked me up at the airport, I met my stepfather. He just said, "Hi, nice to meet you." They showed me my room; my room was so beautiful. It is so beautiful. I was so happy. Then that night, I couldn't sleep. I was really crying a lot. I felt weird in a new home with people that I hadn't lived with for a long time. I know it's my mom, but I . . . I felt weird. I was missing my grandma. I missed the yummy food that my grandma always cooked. I missed the good moments with my grandma when she took me to school. For three nights, I didn't sleep really well. I was crying.

When my mom told me that I was gonna go to school, I was so excited. I was going to have new friends, and I was going to know new people. The school was close to my house, just across the street. The first day my mom went with me, and there were new people, different types of people, like Americans, Chinese guys, and everything. Mexicans and Latino people too. But they knew English, and they just talked to me in English. My first day of school was very bad. People just talked to me, and I didn't understand the things that they said. I didn't know English. Even now, I don't have perfect English. They were talking to me, and everything they said to me was so funny. I always said, "Yes, yes," because I didn't understand. They were always laughing about me. Sometimes I just felt weird between those people.

After I finished middle school, I went to Wellstone High School. It changed everything when I came to Wellstone because they made me feel like family. I have friends that are learning English like me, and I don't feel like the only weird person any more. There are a lot of people that speak Spanish. Latino people that are in the same position as me—they want to learn English. I feel familiar. I feel more comfortable than I did in the middle school, because I know people like me and that they're here to learn. We speak Spanish together, and we try to speak English with the teachers and help each other. I felt really good that year. It was better than the last one.

Right now, I'm still a Wellstone student. I have a lot of friends, a bunch of girlfriends from different kinds of countries . . . Somalia, France—Latino friends, American friends, Mexicans, everything. A year before, I found a job. I'm a cashier at a gas station. I'm good at that. I started working, and I have money now. I feel really happy buying my own things and helping my mom pay the rent and things like that.

I want to have good grades and always try to be better. I want to keep learning. If I learn perfect English, I want to learn another language too, like French, or another one. I want to go to college. The career that I want is very weird, that's what my mom says. I want to be a police officer or something like that. I'm very interested in that. I have an idea of going into the military because I saw some videos and they teach how to protect others.

I already have residency in America, so I'm going to go to Ecuador. I'm so happy because I'm going to see my grandmother again. That's going to be exciting. I went to Ecuador already to see my family, and it was the best time because my grandma reminds me of all the things about my life before.

VIDEO LINKS

greencardvoices.org/speakers/alexandra-irrazabal

Asasa, Ethiopia

Ikrem Nuru

From: Asasa, Ethiopia
Current City: Minneapolis, MN

"YOU DON'T KNOW THE LANGUAGE, THE CULTURE, OR THE PEOPLE. DO EVERYTHING IS NEW FOR YOU. IT'S KIND OF HARD. YOU HAVE TO TAKE YOUR TIME TO GET TO KNOW EVERYTHING."

First of all, I would like to say thank you for letting people know my story. I was born in Ethiopia in a small town called Asasa. I grew up there. I have four brothers and three sisters. I grew up with my mom; my dad left when I was four years old. He left to make our life better. We were seven families, and our house was too small. He went to Kenya. After my dad stayed for four years in Kenya, he got a chance to go to the USA. He worked hard even though he didn't know anyone from the USA. It was hard for him to get to know everyone and the culture, the language, everything. It's just life—life takes you everywhere. He worked hard and then he started sending money, a little money, to Ethiopia. After my dad left, five years later, we bought a huge house. Our lives started changing.

After eight years or something, I can't remember exactly what year, he went back to Ethiopia. He sent a visa for my brothers. They are four years older than me. After my brothers came to America, they started going to school. They were eighteen or something, but now they are twenty or more than twenty. All of them have graduated from high school. One of my brothers graduated from Wellstone. One brother went to college, and the rest of them started working. My older brother bought another house. He bought it there in America.

In 2011, my dad went back to Ethiopia, and he saw us and that me and my sister had grown up, so he sent visas for me and my sister. We came here in 2012. My dad was also trying to bring my sister and my mom. Maybe, if we are fortunate, they will come next year.

In Ethiopia I went to school from grade one to grade eight. I spent my time helping my mom in a little store that she worked in. I also went to dugsi to learn more about my religion. At that time, there was a little fighting, but I did not know exactly why the fighting was happening. The only thing I remember was that people were running around the street, and a few minutes later my mom came to me and took me home. She did not even wear her shoes since she thought someone would kill me, so she ran to protect me from the fighting.

One day I saw my mom was crying, and I asked her why she was crying. She said nothing and she just hugged me and said, "Go to dugsi."

I went to dugsi, and I asked my big sister why mom was crying. My sister said, "I don't know." After we got home, my mom told my neighbor that my dad got a visa for us. She told my neighbors because she knew that we would be unhappy and cry if she told us.

After my neighbor told us that we got visa I said, "Oh, great! Is for four of us?"

Then she said, "No it is just for two of you." I was really shocked when I found out that my mom was not going with us.

My mom told me, "You got your visa; you should go to America."

I said, "What about you?"

She said, "Me and your sister will stay here." I cried because I didn't want to go. She raised us. She is still alone, even though there is a huge house, in that city.

We were supposed to come June 27th. For a while, we just hugged our family, not saying goodbye, not crying. We took so long that the plane left us. We went to the airport, and then we asked the guy. He said, "I'm sorry, your plane already left."

"Oh, what?! So that means we are not going to America anymore?" we said.

"No, no, no, no, you will go tomorrow. It's tomorrow." That time we went on time.

We came to Washington, DC. In DC there was like a big computer in front of us. I thought, "There's a person. She's in the computer, but she's just like us." She was just talking, but I didn't know English. I was like, "Yes," and she kept talking to me! I was like, "No!" I thought she was gonna be quiet, but no. She was just a computer, you know? Not a person. So I was like, "Yes. Blah blah blah blah?"

My sister was like, "It's a computer, who are you talking to? Ikrem, it's a computer!"

I was like, "Oh, really? I thought it was a person." I just laughed. There were a lot of things that happened to us. You know it's hard the first time; you don't know the language, the culture, or the people, so everything is new for you. It's kind of hard. You have to take your time to get to know everything.

When I first arrived, I felt very happy to see my brothers and my father. They had all changed. They grew up and everything was changed. My brother, Amin, he is older than me. When he came here, he was nine years old, and he was too little. But now he's too tall; he looks like twenty-nine, but he's still twenty. I said, "Where's Amin?"

"Here is Amin!" they said.

"No, Amin my brother," I said.

"Here is Amin your brother!"

"Are you guys kidding me?! He is not. Everything about him has changed!" I said. He was still my brother. It just surprised me.

There were just white people around us. I thought, "I am gonna live with all these people?"

My family said, "Oh, you will see people like you in school."

I said, "Okay, we'll see." At first, I went to Lincoln High School, and there were a lot of Somali. Even though we didn't understand the same language, they were not new for me because I had lived with them in my country in Ethiopia.

Now I live with my father. I'm a senior, and I go to MCTC. I hope I will graduate this year and then start going to university or college. I haven't decided yet, but my goal is to become a nurse. I'd love to work in a hospital with the different people there. Also, biology is my favorite subject.

My hope is to continue my education and then to help my dad and mom. They helped me, they got me here, and they gave me everything that I needed. I hope I will work hard and become the person they think. I will change their lives more than this. I would love to say thank you to my mom and dad. They both did great. My father still says, when I say I want to work, "You should continue your school. They can pay you nine dollars or eleven dollars an hour. There is a time when they will give you a hundred. Just continue your school and focus." I listen to him. I've never worked. I have money, like people who work, because every week, every two weeks, he will ask me, "Do you need money?" He will give me fifty or a hundred dollars to buy any clothes I want. So I will say thank you to my dad and mom, who raised me up like what I want to be.

For those people like me, who are immigrants, I would say to continue your education. I know some of them have family issues, and there are students who don't live with their families. Then they start cutting school, and then they start working. But there is a time that you will work and get money, more than you think. Help yourself and then other people. I would say I'd rather have education than money. Because everything has a time. Don't give up on school.

VIDEO LINKS

greencardvoices.org/speakers/ikrem-nuru

Port-au-Prince, Haiti

Wendy Saint-Felix

From: Port-au-Prince, Haiti
Current City: Minneapolis, MN

> "ONE OF MY BIGGEST DREAMS IS TO JOIN THE NAVY ROTC TO BECOME A SEAL AND HAVE SOME GOOD EXPERIENCES THERE. . .I WANT TO PREPARE MY LIFE FOR A BETTER FUTURE AND BRING MY GRANDMOTHER HERE."

I don't have many memories about my life in Haiti, because I was very young. The only thing I can say is that it was very amazing to live in my home country. I lived with my mom, my grandmother, my two sisters, and my uncles. I moved to the Dominican Republic in 2010 after the earthquake in my country. I can say the Dominican Republic was very hard for me at the beginning because I had to learn another language—Spanish. But I went to school, and learned more about this language, and I had many friends there. I think the Dominican Republic is my second home.

I was in school in the morning, and when I came home, my mom said, "We got a visa to go to the United States!"

I said, "Really? When we are going to go?"

"After one month, we're going to go to the United States," she told me.

"Mom, I don't want to go," I said.

"But why?" she asked.

"I have many friends here!"

"But you can make other friends!"

"Yes, but it's difficult for me to learn another language," I said.

"You are smart. You can do that," she told me.

"I'll give it my best," I said. But I didn't want to leave my grandmother. When my mom was not home, she took care of me, and she was crying that day when I went to the airport, saying, "Don't leave me." I was crying too. But I had to do it.

The first week, it was very cold outside. I said, "Mom, what are we doing in this country? It's very cold!"

She told me, "You have to get used to this country."

"I don't want to live here," I said.

"But where would we go?"

"Another country. It's too cold here."

"No," she told me. "We will live here for a while, and maybe after two or three years we can move."

"All right," I said.

The first time I went to downtown, I saw many buildings. I said, "Wow, it's an amazing city."

My mom said to me, "Yeah, you see? It's a good country. You can learn more about this country."

"Alright, I'll try it," I said.

After school, I practice soccer. I'm a soccer player on the Wellstone team. And my life now looks very different from when I first came. I feel more comfortable. My mom, my sisters, and my stepfather care about me and support me a lot. They ask me what I want to do or something. Sometimes I just go alone in my bedroom and think about my grandmother because I miss her a lot. She calls me and asks me how I'm feeling, and I say, "I miss you so much." But we had to leave there, and we have to try to never give up.

In the future . . . first of all, I need to finish my high school and achieve all my goals. One of my biggest dreams is to join the Navy ROTC to become a Seal and have some good experiences there and study while I'm in the Army. I want to prepare my life for a better future and bring my grandmother here.

VIDEO LINKS

greencardvoices.org/speakers/wendy-saint-felix

Borama,
Somalia

Fosiya Hussein

From: Borama, Somalia
Current City: Minneapolis, MN

> "I LIKE TO PLAY BASKETBALL. I WOULD LIKE MANY GIRLS LIKE ME TO BE INTERESTED IN JOINING AS WE NEED MORE GIRLS LIKE ME TO PLAY. SOME GIRLS WOULD LIKE TO PLAY, BUT THEY DON'T HAVE SOMEONE TO HELP THEM SO I LIKE TO DO THAT."

My name is Fosiya Hussein. I was born in Borama, Somalia, in 1996. I have four brothers and four sisters. I am the youngest of my family.

I didn't grow up in Somalia. When I was two or three years old, my family moved to the refugee camp in Ethiopia. We became part of the Somali-Ethiopian community. I went to school in Ethiopia. It was hard to learn my first language in Ethiopia because, in Ethiopia, they speak eighty or more languages. The most important thing that you learn is Amharic. I didn't know Amharic, and I couldn't write the writing. The writing was very hard and speaking was very hard. So I tried to play sports.

After I went to Ethiopia, my oldest sister married an Ethiopian man. I liked the city more before, when I was newcomer, because I got new family and new friends. When I was ten to thirteen, I spent my time going to dugsi and school. When I finished my dugsi, I started to work. I worked with the newcomer refugees to help them get health care.

The day that I got a visa it was September 8th, 2013. Oh . . . that was amazing. How could I feel that day? I never imagined that day, how I would feel, because I would get a new life, a new population, and it would be my third country. I was very happy that day. That day I could have hope to go to America. I waited for the visa for seven years, so I forgot about it and started to finish my last two years in my high school. The day that I got my high school diploma and visa was the same day. I was really feeling happy because I got my wish that I had waited seven years for.

After Ethiopia I went to Phoenix, Arizona. Five of my sisters, my mom, my sister's son, and I went together to Arizona. When I went to Phoenix, my English was bad, and I understood what the people were saying but couldn't repeat it.

The life in Arizona . . . it was good, and I liked it, but it's not good for poor people. When you are new, and you don't know the language, it's hard to get a job. It's hard to communicate. Even when I went to Arizona, I spoke little English. I knew "How are you?", "My name is Fosiya," and "Help me."

Before I started school, I didn't have anything to do. The one thing that I did was look out the window, listening to the noise of cars. Every day I would look out the window, and I saw the neighbors and men who had tattoos. I was scared. I said, "It's dangerous!" because I was new, and back home I never saw a man or woman who had a tattoo. That is why I was scared of everybody that had a tattoo. The things that I did when I was in Arizona were watching people, walking by myself, and going to sleep early. I started high school, but it was a little hard to stay in Arizona because it's too hot.

We came to Minnesota because my family did not have any jobs. Some of my sisters didn't have an education when they were in Arizona. The other reason that we moved was that all the Somali neighborhoods were moving to another state. The reason why all of these people moved from Arizona was that it was hard to get a job, especially for my sisters. They are old and they didn't get an education. They say they needed work. Their English was better than mine. My mom decided to move here, to Minnesota. Some of my relatives told us some information about Minnesota. When my mom looked at Minnesota, she said Minnesota was better than Arizona. And then, in 2014, we moved here.

I live with my mother and three of my sisters. But I hope to be with all of my family someday. Now I go to school at Wellstone International High School. I will graduate this year. Also I go to MCTC and take ESL English. I am very happy. Even after I come back from school, I go to work. It's late but I still have fun with my nephew. Every Friday, all my family goes to the mosque to pray. I am very happy to be there.

I used to play basketball when I was in Africa. I played number three. I liked to shoot the ball. When I came to the United States, I became part of the Wellstone soccer players, but after I got a problem with my foot, I stopped and changed to play basketball. I like to play basketball. I would like many girls like me to be interested in joining as we need more girls like me to play. Some girls would like to play, but they don't have someone to help them so I like to do that. I would like to encourage girls of my age to play basketball.

Still I haven't decided my future goal. I'm not sure yet, but I'm deciding many things; I'm still in high school. I don't know which it would be: nursing or business. One day I decided to go into the military, and I decide everything because the students here tell you everything. They tell you nursing, and they say, "Nursing is good for you!" And then another person says, "Business is good for you because you know math!" I say, when you get the high school diploma, you will decide what you will be.

VIDEO LINKS

greencardvoices.org/speakers/fosiya-hussein

Guadalajara,
Mexico

Eduardo Lopez

From: Guadalajara, Mexico
Current City: Minneapolis, MN

"I USED TO WATCH MOVIES FROM THE UNITED STATES. I REMEMBER ONCE I SAID, 'WHEN I GROWN UP I WANT TO LIVE THERE.'"

When I was three years old, my mom came to the United States. The economy of Mexico is bad. Even if you work every day it's hard to raise a family. You do not get paid enough to have a decent life, and that is why we are here in the United States looking for opportunities. My dad made my mom come to the US. I think my mom did the right thing, even if the right thing was hard. I understand her, because my dad left her and she was by herself, working so that we could have a better life.

I remember when she said, "I'm gonna go first, then you." And I didn't care. I didn't show any feelings when she said that. But when I went home, and she left, then I started crying.

I lived with my grandma for ten years. I went to school there in Mexico, and I met Isidro. I used to call him "father" because my mom and my dad were in the United States. He taught me how to sing and I got into a band. We used to play around the region. Then he died. Ten years later, my mom came back to Mexico, and then we got our green cards, and that's when we came here.

When I first came to the United States, I felt weird, because everything was different from where I come from. But I did want to come here because I used to watch movies from the United States. I remember once I said, "When I grow up I want to live there." I used to feel like I wasn't part of this place, but now I'm used to it. I've been here now for six years.

School was different. I had a hard time socializing with people from here because they're different, and the language is hard. I was kind of antisocial. I used to stay home and just play video games or visit my cousins, but that was it.

I also felt weird living with my mom because she was like someone I just met. I knew she was my mom, but I had not lived with her for a very long time. It was strange; the way we talked or treated each other felt like we were friends, but I did not feel the way I felt about my grandmother. Grandma was the one that raised me and gave me love. It's confusing, but I am sure I love them both. God knows the reasons we go through those challenges. We have to be thankful each day we are alive.

Two years ago, I was really immature. I dropped out of school. I didn't want to study anymore. I don't know what I was thinking. I started working, and at first it was okay, but then I was like, what am I doing with my life? I should go back to school. I realized that school is important. That's why I'm back. If you are not white or at least educated, you do not have another choice but to accept any job with the worst people in the world. Some people are racist and do not see you as an individual. If you educate yourself, you will have better chances to succeed, and you will feel like you fit in any place because you are prepared. "Be the change you want to see in the world."

I want to finish high school. Then I want to go to college and study psychology. I think it's pretty interesting, and I like helping people.

Eduardo Lopez

VIDEO LINKS

greencardvoices.org/speakers/eduardo-lopez

Chiro, Ethiopia

Keriya Hassan

From: Chiro, Ethiopia
Current City: Minneapolis, MN

"THE FIRST WEEK WAS SO WEIRD. I WAS THINKING, 'WHY DID I COME HERE?'"

My life in Ethiopia was good at times, and at times it was not good. I lived there with my family, my whole family—my brothers, my mom, and my sister. I spent my free time with my brothers in the garden. My father got in trouble, and because of that, our lives were in trouble.

They were electing a president and my dad was against them. He wanted to vote for the Oromo president and tell the Oromo people to vote for him. He called a lot of Oromo teenagers to make posters and then they went around the city to convince the people. My father had a flag of Ethiopia, and he put the flag in his office. The police arrested him and decided to kill him because he had that flag. He decided to leave the country because he wanted to survive for us. If they saw him, they were going to kill him. He left the country, and he went to Kenya. After one year, he went to the United States. He sent a visa for us, and we came here.

I remember the time when he called us from the embassy, and my mom told me, "Hey, Keriya, you got a call from embassy." Wow, we were so happy and excited because we never thought we could go to the United States. We were so happy, and then the visa got canceled for two years. We had to stay there and go back to the embassy in two years. Finally they called us and said, "You got the visa," and then we came to America on April 21st, 2013.

When I came to America, there were a lot of people who came to pick us up from the airport. I was so shocked when I came here because I didn't think that all those people would come here to pick us up. When I saw my father, he was changed. He looked different. I hadn't seen him for eight years. He had our pictures when he came to get us because he thought we had changed. We came home. Actually it was not like we expected.

The first week was so weird. I was thinking, "Why did I come here? It would have been better to stay in Ethiopia because my mom is there, even though my father is here. I'm just sitting in the house, doing nothing. If I go out, no one speaks Oromo. They speak a different language. I can't understand that language." And after months and years, I learned it. And I like it.

Now I go to school, and when I go back to my house I work on my homework. I read books and spend my time, my free time, with my little brother. And I have fun. I just stay, go to school, and come back home. On the weekend, I just stay home and go to the library. Sometimes I go shopping.

I haven't decided yet what I will be after I finish high school. I want to be a fashion designer, photographer, and nurse. But I haven't decided which one I could be. And actually, I don't want to go back to Ethiopia in the future; I just want to stay here. And bring my mom.

VIDEO LINKS

greencardvoices.org/speakers/keriya-hassan

Mogadishu,
Somalia

Ahmed Ahmed

From: Mogadishu, Somalia
Current City: Minneapolis, MN

"THAT DAY IT WAS SNOWING, AND I DIDN'T KNOW WHAT IT WAS. I SAID, 'WHERE DOES THIS COME FROM? IS THIS SUGAR OR WHAT?'"

I am from Somalia, but I went to Kenya when I was twelve years old. When I went to Kenya, I went with my family. My family is six brothers and two sisters. When I was in Somalia, I used to go to dugsi. Dugsi is something where you learn Quran. That is mostly what Somali people do when in Somalia. When I went to Kenya, it was my first time studying in school. I played with my friends and went to school there in Kenya. I used to study a lot of subjects. For example, I learned math, English, and IRE, Islamic Religious Education. It was a great town in Kenya. I went to school like two or three years. Then I stopped there, and after one year we moved to Minneapolis, Minnesota in 2012.

The day we got the visa, I was playing with my friends, and one of my family said, "We have to go." And that surprised me. We took two weeks to get ready for our family. But me, I was absent and went to play with my friends.

Finally, one of my big brothers said, "We're going next week."

And I said, "Okay, let's do it." I told my friends, "I'm going to America."

They said, "Good luck. We will see each other again." I was both excited and scared because it was a new country. I didn't have friends in this new country. I miss my friends in Kenya.

When I first came to America, I was feeling like, you know, it was a new place, and everyone was different than I was. When I came to the airport, I saw a lot of people different than everybody, and I said,

125

"Oh, this is a different place." When I saw the sun sometimes, I still thought, "I am in Africa."

First when I came to America, I went to the Somali mall. When I went to the Somali mall, it was like I was still there in Somalia because they were speaking the same language. It made me think of where I was born, and every time I go there I remember Somalia.

That day, it was snowing, and I didn't know what snow was. I'd never seen it before. That was my first time, and I said, "Where does this come from? Is this sugar or what?"

My parents told us, "This is not sugar. This came from the sky. It's like rain." That was a surprise to me.

At first things were hard. How do I take the elevators? How do I know how to open my locker the first time I go to school? My teacher showed me. My friend Mohamed showed me where the library was. He used to take me there and show me how to take the train. I still love to play soccer with my friends. And I love to run. I'm also learning math right now.

I would like to help my family and people who need help in Africa. I would love to help them. I want to go to college. I want to be a professional soccer player. That's my first hope. My second hope is to be an engineer.

VIDEO LINKS

greencardvoices.org/speakers/ahmed-ahmed

Afterword

Introducing ourselves to the students in this book and their stories is just the beginning.

The more important work starts when we engage in difficult but necessary conversations about the changing face of our nation. Immigration plays a significant role in modern America; 1 in 5 Americans speak a language other than English at home. For these reasons, we have included a portion of our Act4Change study guide, a glossary, and links to the students' video narratives, intended to expand the impact of these students' journeys to the United States.

These stories offer an undeniably powerful opportunity for peer to peer learning that we hope to enhance with these resources. The following Act4Change study guide promotes participation scaffolded with thoughtful discussion questions and activities that are designed for hands-on learning, emphasizing personal growth. This guide is an experiential learning tool. It will help teachers, students, and all participants examine their own stories. The study guide is intended to be used in a variety of settings. For example, it can be used in schools within or across grade levels, reading groups or book clubs, and even between different schools.

We hope that these tools spark deeply meaningful conversations about identity, appreciation of difference, and our shared human experience.

If you would like an extended version of the study guide or to learn about educator workshops on how to use the Act4Change study guide, visit our website—*www.greencardvoices.org.*

Act4Change
A Green Card Voices Study Guide

Each person has the power to tell their own story in their own voice. The art of storytelling translates across cultures and over time. In order to learn about and appreciate voices other than our own, we must be exposed to and given tools to foster an understanding of a variety of voices. We must be able to view the world from others' perspectives in order to act as agents of change in today's world.

Green Card Youth Voices is comprised of the inspirational voices from a young group of recent immigrants to the US that can be shared with a wide audience. This study guide will provide readers with questions to help them explore universal themes, such as storytelling, immigration, identity, and perspective.

Introduce New Voices:
Participants will select one of the twenty-one storytellers featured in *Green Card Youth Voices* and adopt that person's story as his or her own "new voice." For example, one participant may choose Farhat Sadat while another might choose Mario. Participants will become familiar with the life story of their "new voice" and develop a personal connection to it. After each participant has chosen his or her "new voice," read the personal essay first and then watch the video.

Act4Change 1 :
Answer the following questions—
1. Why did you select the storyteller that you did?
2. What was interesting to you about his/her story?
3. What do you and the storyteller have in common?
4. What have you learned as a result of reading/listening to this person's story?

Learn About New Voices 1:

Divide participants into groups of three or four people. Provide each group with copies of the written narratives from five selected stories. Each person within each group will read one of the five narratives. Once finished, the participants will share their narratives with the others. Then, as a group, choose one of the five "voices" and watch that person's video.

Afterward, go on to the journal activity below.

Act4Change 2:
Answer the following questions—

1. What new information about immigrants did you learn from this second storyteller?
2. Compare and contrast the storyteller's video to his/her story. Which did you prefer? Why?
3. What are some similarities between you and the second storyteller?
4. If this really was your "new voice," what might you want to know about America upon arriving?
5. If you could only bring one suitcase on your move to another country, what would you pack in it? Why?

Learn About New Voices 2:

Each participant will be given a third "new voice," and only one can go to each student; there can be no duplicates.

Inform participants not to share the identity of their "new voice." Participants will try to match their classmates' "new voices" to one of the stories in the book. Encourage participants to familiarize themselves with all of the voices featured in *Green Card Youth Voices*.

Act4Change 3:

1. After they are given their "new voice," ask participants to try and create connections between this third voice and themselves. Have the students read their story and then watch the video of their "new voice." Have them think of a piece of art, dance, song, spokenword, comic, sculpture, or other medium of their choosing that best describes their "new voice."

2. Participants will present a 3-5 minute artistic expression for the larger group from the perspective of their "new voice" in thirty-five minutes. The audience will have a template with a chart that includes each of the thirty GCYV students' names, their photo, and a one- or two-sentence abbreviated biography. Audience members will use this chart throughout the activities to keep track of what has been learned about each voice that they have heard.

3. Ask the participants to describe the relationship between the Green Card Youth Voices and themselves:

   a. What did you notice about the form of artistic expression and the story?

   b. What drew you to this specific art form?

   c. Do you notice any cultural relationships between the "new voice" and the piece of art that was chosen?

   d. What is your best advice to immigrant students on how to succeed in this country? State? City?

More than Meets the Eye:

In small groups, have participants read and watch three or four selected narratives from *Green Card Youth Voices*. After that, have group members tell each other facts about themselves and tell the others in the group what they would not know just by looking at them. For example, participants can share an interesting talent, a unique piece of family history, or a special interest. Then have group members discuss things that they found surprising about the students in *Green Card Youth Voices*.

Think about the "new voice" you transformed in Act4Change 3. Tell your group something that was "more than meets the eye" from the perspective of that "new voice!"

For the complete version of *Act4Change: A Green Card Voices Study Guide,* visit our website—www.greencardvoices.org

See also:

Act4Change: A Green Card Youth Voices Study Guide, Workshop for Educators
This workshop is a focused learning experience crafted to deepen teacher understanding and provide instructional strategy, particularly designed to be used in conjunction with *Green Card Youth Voices.*

Glossary

Al-Shabaab: Al Qaeda affiliate located in Somalia.

Amharic: the dominant language of Ethiopia; Semitic origin.

Appeal: an application for review of an alleged injustice.

Basico: middle school in Guatemala.

The Beast: also known as "La Bestia" refers to a network of Mexican freight trains that are utilized by US- bound migrants to more quickly traverse the length of Mexico.

Burra: Spanish word meaning stupid, silly, uncultured, an insult; literally means donkey.

Caseworker: a person appointed to oversee the status of a refugee.

Chuzos: Ecuadorian thin beef skewers or meat on a stick.

Cristiano: Cristiano Ronaldo is a world famous, Portuguese soccer player.

Dadaab: the location of a refugee camp in Kenya.

Doha: the capital city of Qatar.

Dubai: the most populous city in the United Arab Emirates.

Dugsi: a Somali word for school.

Extortionist: a criminal who extracts money from a disadvantaged party.

ESL: English as a Second Language.

Green card: a commonly used name for a Lawful Permanent Resident Card. Generally denotes that the person carrying it has Lawful Permanent Resident status.

Guía: "guide" in Spanish.

Hijab: head scarf worn by some Muslim women.

Inshallah: a phrase from Arabic meaning "if Allah wills it" or "God willing."

IOM: the International Organization for Migration.

Juvenile detention: the temporary custody of young people whose alleged conduct is subject to court jurisdiction.

Kakuma: a town in the Northwestern region of Kenya.

Lottery: a drawing of chance that selects people to receive diversity visas for the US.

MCTC: Minneapolis Community & Technical College.

Nakuru: a major city in Kenya.

Orientation (in refugee camps): education on the customs of a country, in this case the US.

Oromo people: Ethiopia's largest ethnic group.

Refugee: a person who is outside their country of residence or nationality who is unable or unwilling to return and unable and unwilling to avail herself or himself of the protection of their original country of residence or nationality because of persecution or a well-founded fear of persecution on account of race, religion, nationality, membership in a particular social group, or political opinion.

Refugee camp: temporary housing for people displaced by warfare or religious or political reasons.

Seco de pollo: Ecuadorian chicken stew.

Sheder: a refugee camp in Ethiopia.

STEP-UP: a nationally recognized youth employment model that trains and matches Minneapolis youth ages 14–21 with paid summer internships.

Tonta: Someone of low intelligence, making ridiculous errors in judgement

Upward Bound Vision Quest: a college access program at the University of Minnesota funded by the US Department of Education.

Visa: a physical stamp in the passport, or document granted by a US Embassy or Consulate outside the US, that permits the recipient to approach the US border and request permission to enter the US in a particular immigrant or nonimmigrant status.

Visa process: a nonimmigrant or immigrant application submitted to the U.S. Embassy or Consulate to obtain an immigrant or nonimmigrant visa.

About Green Card Voices

Founded in 2013, Green Card Voices is a Minneapolis-based, nationally growing social enterprise that works to record and share first person narratives of America's immigrants to facilitate a better understanding between immigrant and non-immigrant communities. Our dynamic, multimedia platform, book collections, and traveling exhibits are designed to empower a variety of educational institutions, community groups, and individuals to acquire first-person perspectives about immigrants' lives, increasing the appreciation of the immigrant experience in America.

Green Card Voices was born from the idea that the broad narrative of current immigrants should be communicated in a way that is true to each immigrant's story. We seek to be a new lens for those in the immigration dialogue and to build a bridge between immigrants and nonimmigrants— newcomers and the receiving community—from across the country. We do this by sharing the firsthand immigration stories of foreign-born Americans, and by helping others to see the "wave of immigrants" as individuals with interesting stories of family, hard work, and cultural diversity.

To date, the Green Card Voices team has recorded the life stories of over three hundred immigrants coming from more than one hundred different countries. All immigrants who decide to share their story with GCV are asked six open-ended questions. In addition, they are asked to share personal photos of their life in their country of birth and in the US. The recorded narratives are edited down to five-minute videos filled with personal photographs, an intro, an outro, captions, and background music. These video stories are available on www.greencardvoices.org, and YouTube (free of charge and advertising).

Immigration Stories from a Minneapolis High School was the first book to be published in the *Green Card Youth Voices* series. It was joined by similar publications featuring stories from high school students in Fargo, St. Paul, and Atlanta. Green Card Voices has also published *Green Card Entrepreneur Voices: How-To Business Stories from Minnesota Immigrants*.

Contact information:
www.greencardvoices.org
info@greencardvoices.org • 612.889.7635

Facebook: www.facebook.com/GreenCardVoices
Twitter: www.twitter.com/GreenCardVoices

Immigrant Youth Traveling Exhibits

Twenty students' stories from each city in the *Green Card Youth Voices* series (Minneapolis, Fargo, and St. Paul) are featured in traveling exhibits, available to schools, universities, libraries, and other venues where communities gather. Each exhibit features twenty stories from a particular city, each with a portrait, a 200-word biography, and a quote from each immigrant. A QR code is displayed next to each portrait and can be scanned with a mobile device to watch the digital stories. The following programming can be provided with the exhibit: panel discussions, presentations, and community-building events.

Green Card Voices currently has six exhibits based on different communities across the Midwest. To rent an exhibit, please contact us at 612.889.7635 or info@greencardvoices.org.

Green Card Youth Voices: Book Readings

Meeting the student authors in person creates a dynamic space in which to engage with these topics firsthand. Book readings are a wonderful opportunity to hear the students share their stories and answer questions about their lived experiences.

To schedule a book reading in your area, please contact us at 612.889.7635 or info@greencardvoices.org.

Also Available:
Green Card Entrepreneur Voices:
How-To Business Stories from Minnesota Immigrants

This is a collection of essays and digital narratives from twenty immigrant and refugee entrepreneurs living in Minnesota. These storytellers come from nineteen different countries. Written in the tellers' own words, these stories offer insight into immigrant entrepreneur expertise: how they did it, why they did it, and what they learned in the process. Available as an ebook (ISBN: 978-1-949523-09-6 and paperback (ISBN: 978-1-949523-07-2).

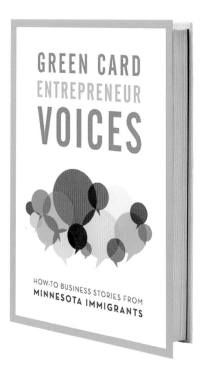

Contents:

- Full color portraits
- 19 personal essays written by Minnesotan entrepreneurs
- Links to digital video stories on the Green Card Voices website
- Forward by Dr. Rajiv Tandon, President of The Institute for Innovators and Entrepreneurs at Hamline University
- Glossary

To purchase online and view a list of retailers, visit greencardvoices.org/books.

Also available on Amazon.

Green Card Youth Voices:
Immigration Stories from an Atlanta High School

This book is a collection of twenty-one personal essays written by refugee and immigrant students, and one teacher from Cross Keys High School Clarkston High School and DeKalb International Student Center in Atlanta, Georgia. The young storytellers—including six DACA recipients—come from nineteen different countries and reveal in their own words the complexity and humanity of the immigration experience that is too often obscured in current conversations. Available as an ebook (ISBN: 978-1-949523-08-9) and paperback (ISBN : 978-1-949523-05-8).

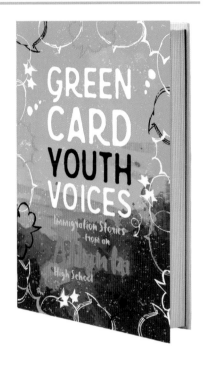

Contents:

- Full color portraits
- 21 personal essays by students from around the world
- Links to digital video stories on the Green Card Voices website
- Foreword by Luma Mufleh, Founder and CEO of Fugees Family, Inc. and Head Coach of the Fugees Soccer Teams
- Excerpt from *Act4Change: A Green Card Voices Study Guide*
- Glossary

Also available:
Green Card Youth Voices:
Immigration Stories from a Fargo High School

Based on the successful model used in Minneapolis, *Green Card Youth Voices: Immigration Stories from a Fargo High School* features thirty-one authors from Fargo South High School. These are the memories, realities, and hopes of young people from twenty-seven different countries, who were brought together into one classroom. The stories in this book highlight the resilience, bravery, and courage that these new Americans have gained. Available as an ebook (ISBN: 978-1-949523-03-4) and paperback (ISBN : 978-1-949523-02-7).

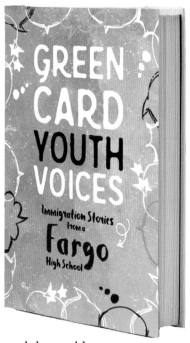

Contents:

- Full color portraits
- 31 personal essays by students from around the world
- Links to digital video stories on the Green Card Voices website
- Forward by Betty Gronneberg, Founder & Executive Director of uCodeGirl and author of *The Alphabet Takes a Journey: Destination Ethiopia*
- Excerpt from *Act4Change: A Green Card Voices Study Guide*
- Glossary

2017 Foreword INDIES Finalist for
Young Adult Nonfiction

2018 Gold Medal Winner for
Best Regional Nonfiction

To purchase online and view a list of retailers,
visit greencardvoices.org/books.

Also available on Amazon.

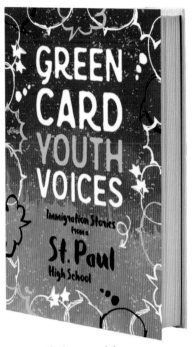

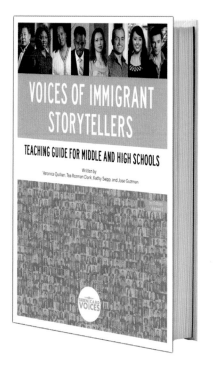